Pocket
MADRID
TOP SIGHTS • LOCAL LIFE • MADE EASY

Anthony Ham

In This Book

QuickStart Guide

Your keys to understanding the city – we help you decide what to do and how to do it

Need to Know
Tips for a smooth trip

Neighbourhoods
What's where

Explore Madrid

The best things to see and do, neighbourhood by neighbourhood

Top Sights
Make the most of your visit

Local Life
The insider's city

The Best of Madrid

The city's highlights in handy lists to help you plan

Best Walks
See the city on foot

Madrid's Best...
The best experiences

Survival Guide

Tips and tricks for a seamless, hassle-free city experience

Getting Around
Travel like a local

Essential Informatio
Including where to sta

Our selection of the city's best places to eat, drink and experience:

◉ **Sights**

✕ **Eating**

🍷 **Drinking**

✰ **Entertainment**

🛍 **Shopping**

These symbols give you the vital information for each listing:

☎ Telephone Numbers	👪 Family-Friendly	
⊘ Opening Hours	🐾 Pet-Friendly	
🅿 Parking	🚌 Bus	
✤ Nonsmoking	⛴ Ferry	
@ Internet Access	Ⓜ Metro	
🛜 Wi-Fi Access	Ⓢ Subway	
🌱 Vegetarian Selection	🚃 Tram	
🍽 English-Language Menu	🚆 Train	

Find each listing quickly on maps for each neighbourhood:

Bar Hemingway

16 🍷 Map p233, B2

Legend has it that Hemi self, wielding a machine rate this timber-pan ered bar during showpiece is a en by Papa ar town. Dress s.com; Hôtel Rit ⊘ 6.30pm-2a

6 ◉ Plac

Lonely Planet's Madrid

Lonely Planet Pocket Guides are designed to get you straight to the heart of the city.

Inside you'll find all the must-see sights, plus tips to make your visit to each one really memorable. We've split the city into easy-to-navigate neighbourhoods and provided clear maps so you'll find your way around with ease. Our expert authors have searched out the best of the city: walks, food, nightlife and shopping, to name a few. Because you want to explore, our 'Local Life' pages will take you to some of the most exciting areas to experience the real madrid.

And of course you'll find all the practical tips you need for a smooth trip: itineraries for short visits, how to get around, and how much to tip the guy who serves you a drink at the end of a long day's exploration.

It's your guarantee of a really great experience.

Our Promise

You can trust our travel information because Lonely Planet authors visit the places we write about, each and every edition. We never accept freebies for positive coverage, so you can rely on us to tell it like it is.

QuickStart Guide

Welcome to Madrid

No city on earth is more alive than Madrid, a beguiling place whose sheer energy carries a simple message: this is one city that knows how to live. Madrid's calling cards are many: astonishing art galleries, stunning architecture, relentless nightlife, fine restaurants and tapas bars. Other cities have some of these things. Madrid has them all in bucketloads.

Tapas bar, Mercado de San Miguel (p32)
MATTES RENÃ/GETTY IMAGES ©

Madrid
Top Sights

Museo del Prado (p66)
Spain's premier art gallery is also one of Europe's finest, an extraordinary co
lection that ranges from Goya and Velázquez to Rembrandt, Rubens and Bo
If you visit one Madrid art gallery, make it the Museo del Prado.

Centro de Arte Reina Sofía (p72)

Where the Prado gathers together the old masters, the Reina Sofía is all about contemporary art, with Picasso, Dalí and Miró leading the way. Picasso's *Guernica* alone is worth the admission price 10 times over.

Museo Thyssen-Bornemisza (p76)

The third pillar of Madrid's triumvirate of stellar art museums, the Thyssen's private collection is a staggering journey through the best in European art. There's scarcely a European master that doesn't make an appearance here.

Parque del Buen Retiro (p80)

This glorious and expansive parkland was once a royal hideaway, but it's now one of our favourite places in Madrid to picnic and wander amid the abundant greenery, water and beautiful monuments.

Plaza Mayor (p24)

In this city of pretty public squares, the Plaza Mayor is easily the most picturesque, combining stately architecture, a compelling history and the rich canvas of modern Madrid life.

Ermita de San Antonio de la Florida (p114)

Tucked away from Madrid's tourist heartland, this tiny hermitage contains a magnificent secret: vivid frescoes adorning the domes just as Goya painted them more than two centuries ago.

Palacio Real (p26)

Madrid's royal palace provides the backdrop to some of the city's loveliest urban views, but the interior is a lavish study in Spanish royal extravagance down through the centuries.

San Lorenzo de El Escorial (p118)

Away in the cool, mountain foothills northwest of Madrid, this palace-monastery complex is a monument worthy of the aspirations to greatness of many a Spanish king. It's also one of Madrid's most rewarding day trips.

Museo Lázaro Galdiano (p86)

One of numerous elegant mansions in the upmarket neighbourhood of Salamanca, this fine stately home is one of Madrid's most eclectic collections of curios mixed in with artworks of the highest calibre.

Plaza de Toros & Museo Taurino (p98)

Spain's spiritual home of bullfighting hosts *corridas* (bullfights) from May to October, but is always worth visiting for Moorish architecture, the fascinating museum and guided tours that takes you inside this peculiarly Spanish passion.

Madrid
Local Life

Insider tips to help you find the real

If you're looking for the perfect complement to Madrid's major sights, we introduce you to five routes through the city's neighbourhoods that show you how experience Madrid like a local.

Sunday at El Rastro (p40)

▶ Shopping
▶ Tapas and vermouth

Visiting the Sunday morning flea market of El Rastro is a Madrid institution. It tumbles down the hill from La Latina to Lavapiés, and, this being Madrid, it's always followed by a tapas and vermouth crawl through the bars of La Latina.

A Night Out in Huertas (p52)

▶ Classy bars, classic bars
▶ Great live music

Huertas is the city's true hub of after-dark action. Gorgeous Plaza de Santa Ana is the focal point around which so much

of the energy swirls, but the surrounding streets are filled with old bars that haven't changed in decades, rooftop bars for urban sophisticates, fabulous live-music venues and outstanding nightclubs.

Shopping in Upmarket Salamanca (p88)

▶ High fashion
▶ Gourmet food

Salamanca is the epicentre of Spain's world-renowned fashion industry. Calle de Serrano and surrounds are where the locals shop in boutiques of Spanish designers while the elite track down the most prestigious

international labels. Gourmet food shops tapas bars where foo art fit perfectly in th stylish surrounds.

Counterculture i Malasaña (p102)

▶ An alternative slant
▶ Vintage Madrid

Salamanca's alter eg down-and-dirty Mala is where heady 1980 drid lives and breath It's all about retro fa ions, fine old cafes a nightlife where dress down is the done thi and about street cre and a local clientele effortlessly spans the spectrum from ageing *rockeros* to Madrid's young things.

Plaza de Santa Ana (p50)

io Life in
mberí (p116)

itional and authentic
sic shops and bars
derstand what
s Madrid tick,
a few hours in
berí just north
centre. With
uing sights to
or your visit, au-
icity is otherwise
ey with fine old
, classic *barrio*
nd the Plaza de
de, one of our
rite little squares
city.

KRZYSZTOF DYDYNSKI/GETTY IMAGES ©

El Rastro Sunday market (p40)

Madrid
Day Planner

Day One

So many Madrid days begin in the **Plaza Mayor** (p24), or perhaps nearby with a breakfast of *chocolate con churros* at **Chocolatería de San Ginés** (p34). While you're in the old town, drop by the **Plaza de la Villa** (p30) and **Plaza de Oriente** (p30).

Stop for a coffee or wine at **Cafe de Oriente** (p34), visit the **Palacio Real** (p26), then graze on tapas for lunch at the **Mercado de San Miguel** (p32). If you've only time to visit one Madrid art gallery, make it the peerless **Museo del Prado** (p66), where you could easily spend an entire afternoon. Wander down the Paseo del Prado to admire **Caixa Forum** (p83), before climbing up through the narrow lanes of Huertas to a pre-dinner tipple at **La Venencia** (p58).

Dinner at **Restaurante Sobrino de Botín** (p32) is a fine way to spend your evening and an experience you'll always remember. Perhaps take in a flamenco show at **Las Tablas** (p35), followed by a cocktail at **Museo Chicote** (p109). If you're up for a long night, **Teatro Joy Eslava** (p35) is an icon of the Madrid night.

Day Two

Get to the **Centro de Arte Reina Sofía** (p72) early to be[at] the crowds, then, after the clamour [of] yesterday, climb up through sedate s[...] to spend a couple of hours soaking u[p] the calm of the **Parque del Buen Re[tiro]** (p80).

Wander down to admire the **P[laza] de la Cibeles** (p83), have an[d] tapas lunch at **Estado Puro** (p83) or [Los] **Gatos** (p57), then catch the Metro ac[ross] town to admire the Goya frescoes in [the] **Ermita de San Antonio de la Florid[a]** (p114). Back in town, shop for souven[irs] **Casa de Diego** (p61), **El Arco Artesa[no]** (p37) and **Antigua Casa Talavera** (p[...]) before heading to **Café del Real** (p34[)] a drink. Then it's on to Plaza de Santa [Ana] for another drink, or three, at an outd[oor] table if the weather's fine.

Check out if there's live jazz o[n] offer at wonderful **Café Centr[al]** (p60), then have an after-show drink [at] **Imperfecto** (p59), then dinner at **Vi C[...]** (p56) or **Casa Alberto** (p56), depend[ing] on your mood. The night is still young[.] **Kapital** (p83) is good if you're in the [mood] to dance, **La Terraza del Urban** (p59[) if] you're in need of more sybaritic pleas[ure].

on time?

arranged Madrid's must-sees into these day-by-day itineraries to make
ou see the very best of the city in the time you have available.

Three

Spend the morning at the third of
Madrid's world-class art galleries,
useo Thyssen-Bornemisza (p76),
ead out east to take a tour of the
de Toros (p98) bullring, before
ling the rest of the morning shop-
along Calle de Serrano.

If you're feeling extravagant, try
lunch at **Sula Madrid** (p93);
ve fallen in love with the idea of
, lunch instead at **Biotza** (p94) and
lonial de Goya** (p93). After lunch,
an hour or two at the **Museo**
o Galdiano** (p86), before dropping
the hill for a coffee at the storied
Restaurante El Espejo (p111).

As dusk approaches, catch the
metro across town to La Latina
pend as long as you can picking
vay among the tapas bars of Calle
Cava Baja. A wine at **Taberna**
ranillo** (p47) and a mojito out on
de la Paja at **Delic** (p41) should set
o for the night ahead. Live music is
at way to spend it, either at **Sala El**
060) or **Costello Café & Niteclub**
. Then lose all sense of decorum
ng the night away at **Why Not?**
) in Chueca.

Day Four

☼ If you really love your art, an hour
or two in the morning at **Real
Academia de Bellas Artes de San
Fernando** (p55) will nicely round out your
experience of Madrid's exceptional art
scene. You've been around almost long
enough to be a local and it's therefore
worth exploring the laneways of Malasaña
between Calle Pez, Plaza Dos de Mayo
and the Glorieta de Bilbao – stop off at
Lolina Vintage Café (p103) along Calle
del Espíritu Santo, **Café Manuela** (p109)
on Calle de San Vincente Ferrer, and **Café
Comercial** (p109).

☼ Lunch at **Albur** (p107), **Nina**
(p107) or **La Musa** (p106) along
Calle de Manuela Malasaña. If you've left
a minimum of three hours to play with,
take a train out of town to **San Lorenzo
de El Escorial** (p118) to enjoy the clear
mountain air and lavish palace-monastery
complex.

☾ Back in town, if you've timed your
run well, you've time for one last
performance, this time *zarzuela* at **Teatro
de la Zarzuela** (p60). Your last night
deserves a special meal – try **La Terraza
del Casino** (p57) to really be blown away,
although you'll need to have booked well in
advance. To round out your visit, hit **Cool**
(p36), **Almonte** (p95) or **El Junco Jazz
Club** (p111), depending on what sort of
memories you'd like to leave Madrid with.

Need to Know

**For more information,
see Survival Guide (p145)**

Currency
Euro (€)

Language
Spanish (Castellano)

Visas
Generally not required for stays of up to 90 days (not at all for members of EU or Schengen countries). Some nationalities need a Schengen visa.

Money
ATMs widely available. Credit cards accepted in most hotels, restaurants and shops.

Mobile Phones
Local SIM cards widely available and can be used in European and Australian mobile phones. Other phones may need to be set to roaming.

Time
Western European (GMT/UTC plus one hour during winter, plus two hours during daylight-saving period)

Plugs & Adaptors
Plugs have two round pins; electrical current is 220V/230V.

Tipping
Small change (€1 per person in restaurants) and rounding up (in taxis) is usually sufficient.

❶ Before You Go

Your Daily Budget

Budget less than €80
▶ Dorm beds €15–20; *hostal* (budget doubles €50–70

▶ Three-course *menú del día* lunches

▶ Plan sightseeing around 'free admiss times

Midrange €80–200
▶ Double room in midrange hotel €75–

▶ Lunch and/or dinner in decent resta

▶ Use discount cards to keep costs dov

Top End more than €200
▶ Double room in top-end hotel from €

▶ Fine dining for lunch and dinner

Useful Websites

EsMadrid.com (www.esmadrid.com) To office's website.

LeCool (www.lecool.com) Alternative, c and avant-garde.

Lonely Planet (www.lonelyplanet.com /madrid) An overview of Madrid with hu dreds of useful links.

Turismo Madrid (www.turismomadrid. es) Regional Comunidad de Madrid tou office site.

Advance Planning

Three months Reserve your hotel as e as you can.

One month Book a table at Sergi Arol Gastro (www.sergiarola.es), La Terraza Casino (www.casinodemadrid.es) or Viridiana (www.restauranteviridiana.c

One week Book online entry to the M del Prado (www.museodelprado.es) t avoid queues on arrival.

Arriving in Madrid

visitors arrive at Aeropuerto de Bara-
km northeast of the city. There are
rminals: T4 is separated from the
, but connected by bus and metro.
ravellers will arrive at either
artín or Atocha stations.

Aeropuerto de Barajas

ination	Best Transport
Mayor & Royal id	EMT Airport Bus & metro (line 2)
anta Ana & tas	EMT Airport Bus & metro (line 2)
tina & iés	EMT Airport Bus & metro (line 2)
tiro & rt Museums	EMT Airport Bus
saña & Chueca	Metro (lines 8 & 10)

Estación de Atocha

ination	Best Transport
Mayor & Royal id	Metro (line 1)
anta Ana & tas	Metro (line 1)
tina & Lavapiés	Metro (lines 1 & 5)
tiro & the Art ums	Walk
saña & Chueca	Metro (lines 1 & 5)

Estación de Chamartín

ination	Best Transport
Mayor & Royal id	Metro (line 1)
anta Ana & tas	Metro (line 1)
tina & Lavapiés	Metro (lines 1 & 5)
tiro & the Art ums	Metro (lines 1 & 2)
saña & Chueca	Metro (lines 5 & 10)

3 Getting Around

Madrid has an efficient and comprehensive
public transport system. Easily the best
way to get around town is by the metro, an
excellent network that covers the whole city.
The bus system is also outstanding. Conven-
iently, both operate under the same ticketing
system; it works out cheaper to purchase
the ten-trip Metrobus ticket (€12) than individual tickets. If you know your address and
the address of where you want to go, visit
the website of the Sistema de Información
de Transportes de Madrid (www.ctm-madrid
.es/como_ir_a/madrid/como_ir_a_madrid1
.jsp) to find the quickest way to get there.

M Metro

Twelve colour-coded metro lines criss-cross
central Madrid (www.metromadrid.es),
although only numbers 1 to 10 are likely to
be of use to travellers. All Madrid neighbourhoods have convenient stations, and the
only place you're likely to need to walk any
distance (and it's a lovely walk!) to get where
you need to go is along Paseo del Prado, with
metro stations at either end.

Bus

Madrid's EMT bus network nicely comple-
ments the metro and lets you see the city as
you travel around. Visit www.emtmadrid.es
for route maps and numbers.

Cercanías Trains

The short-range *cercanías* regional trains
operated by Renfe (www.renfe.es/cercanias
/madrid) go as far afield as El Escorial,
and they can be handy for making a quick,
north–south hop between Chamartín and
Atocha train stations (with stops at Nuevos
Ministerios and Sol).

Madrid
Neighbourhoods

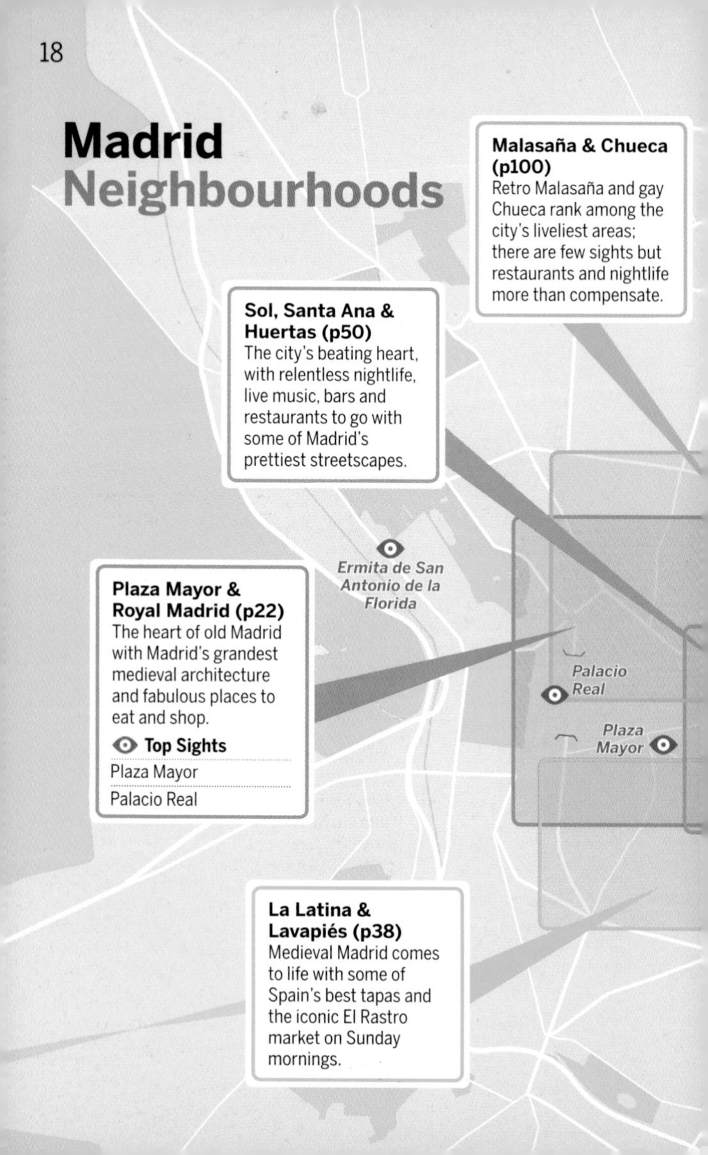

Malasaña & Chueca (p100)
Retro Malasaña and gay Chueca rank among the city's liveliest areas; there are few sights but restaurants and nightlife more than compensate.

Sol, Santa Ana & Huertas (p50)
The city's beating heart, with relentless nightlife, live music, bars and restaurants to go with some of Madrid's prettiest streetscapes.

Ermita de San Antonio de la Florida

Plaza Mayor & Royal Madrid (p22)
The heart of old Madrid with Madrid's grandest medieval architecture and fabulous places to eat and shop.

◉ Top Sights

Plaza Mayor

Palacio Real

Palacio Real ◉

Plaza Mayor ◉

La Latina & Lavapiés (p38)
Medieval Madrid comes to life with some of Spain's best tapas and the iconic El Rastro market on Sunday mornings.

Museo Lázaro Galdiano

Worth a Trip
👁 Top Sights
Plaza de Toros & Museo Taurino

Ermita de San Antonio de la Florida

San Lorenzo de El Escorial

👁 **Plaza de Toros & Museo Taurino**

Salamanca (p84)
Upmarket, quiet neighbourhood; fine boutiques, designer tapas bars and trendy food stores make this Madrid's home of style.

👁 Top Sights
Museo Lázaro Galdiano

Museo Thyssen-Bornemisza

Parque del Buen Retiro

Museo del Prado

Centro de Arte Reina Sofía

El Retiro & the Art Museums (p64)
Spain's golden mile of art with a glorious park thrown in.
👁 Top Sights
Museo del Prado

Centro de Arte Reina Sofía

Museo Thyssen-Bornemisza

Parque del Buen Retiro

Explore
Madrid

Worth a Trip

Plaza Mayor (p24)
SANDRA RACCANELLO/SIME/4CORNERS ©

Explore

Plaza Mayor & Royal Madrid

From the heart of old Madrid to the city's historical seat of royal power, here is Madrid's story at its most grand. This is where the city's tale began and a palpable sense of history survives in the tangled laneways that open onto elegant squares, all watched over by monasteries, churches and the grand public buildings that define old Spain.

e Sights in a Day

Begin with breakfast on **Plaza de Oriente** (p30) at **Cafe de** **iente** (p34), then beat the crowds by ing the **Palacio Real** (p26) when ens. Pause at the **cathedral** (p31) Muralla Árabe (Arab Wall), then b Calle Mayor to **Plaza de la Villa**), which is home to distinctive drid architecture. **Convento de las calzas Reales** (p30) is open only e morning and is not to be missed. ch at the **Mercado de San Miguel**).

Linger for as long as you can in **Plaza Mayor** (p24), perhaps wsing the high-quality souvenirs l Arco Artesanía (p37) before dering down to the **Iglesia de San** **és** (p31), followed by a lazy after-n mojito at **Café del Real** (p34); if can get one of the upstairs tables he window, you'll stay here longer n planned.

A busy night begins with flamenco at **Café de Chinitas**) or **Las Tablas** (p35), followed meal at **Restaurante Sobrino de n** (p32). **Anticafé** (p35) is good for t drinks, followed by all-night cing at **Teatro Joy Eslava** (p35). t around the corner, stop for *choco-con churros* at **Chocolatería de Ginés** (p34) on the way home.

Getting There

M Metro Sol is the most conven-ient station with lines 1, 2 and 3 all passing through. Ópera (lines 2 and 5) is right in the heart of the neighbourhood.

M Metro Other stations around the periphery include Plaza de España (lines 3 and 10), Callao (1, 3 and 5) and La Latina (5).

Top Sights
Plaza Mayor

It's easy to fall in love with Madrid in the Plaza Mayor. This is the monumental heart of the city and the grand stage for so many of the city's most important historical events. Here, Madrid's relentless energy courses across its cobblestones beneath ochre-hued apartments, wrought-iron balconies, frescoes and stately spires. This juxtaposition of endlessly moving city life and more static architectural attractions is typical of the city.

👁 Map p28, D6

Plaza Mayor

Ⓜ Sol

Equestrian statue of Felipe III, Plaza Mayor

n't Miss

tory's Tale

gned in 1619 by Juan Gómez de Mora and
t in typical Herrerian style, of which the slate
es are the most obvious expression, Plaza
or's first public ceremony was the beatifica-
of San Isidro Labrador (St Isidro the Farm
urer), Madrid's patron saint. Bullfights, often
elebration of royal weddings or births, with
lty watching on from the balconies and up
0,000 people crammed into the plaza, were a
rring theme until 1878. Far more notorious
e the *autos-da-fé* (the ritual condemnations of
tics during the Spanish Inquisition) followed
xecutions – burnings at the stake and deaths
arrotte on the north side of the square, hang-
to the south.

l Casa de la Panadería

warm colours of the apartments with their
wrought-iron balconies are offset by the ex-
ite frescoes of the 17th-century **Real Casa de
anadería** (Royal Bakery). The present fres-
date to just 1992 and are the work of artist
os Franco, who chose images from the signs
e zodiac and gods (eg Cybele) to provide a
ning backdrop for the plaza. The frescoes
inaugurated to coincide with Madrid's 1992
as European Capital of Culture.

pe III

e middle of the square stands an eques-
statue of the man who ordered the plaza's
struction: Felipe III. Originally placed in the
a de Campo (M Batán), it was moved to Plaza
or in 1848, whereafter it became a favoured
ting place for irreverent *madrileños* who ar-
ed to catch up 'under the balls of the horse'.

☑ **Top Tips**

▶ To see the plaza's epic
history told in pictures,
check out the carvings
on the circular seats
beneath the lamp posts.

▶ On Sunday mornings,
the plaza's arcaded
perimeter is taken over
by traders of old coins,
banknotes and stamps.

▶ In December and
early January the plaza is
occupied by a Christ-
mas market selling the
season's kitsch.

▶ The bars and restau-
rants with outdoor tables
spilling onto the plaza
are often overpriced and
best avoided.

✗ **Take a Break**

Just beyond the
square's western pe-
rimeter, the Mercado
de San Miguel (p32)
combines historical
architecture with one of
Madrid's most exciting
eating experiences.

For fast food Madrid
style, drop down off
the plaza's south-
eastern corner for a
bocadillo de calamares
(a roll filled with deep-
fried calamari) at Bar
La Ideal (p34).

Top Sights
Palacio Real

You can almost imagine how the eyes of Felipe V, the first of the Bourbon kings, lit up when the *alcázar* (Muslim-era fortress) burned down in 1734 on Madrid's most exclusive perch of real estate. His plan? Build a palace that would dwarf all its European counterparts. The resulting 2800-room royal palace never quite attained such a scale, but it's still an Italianate baroque architectural landmark of arresting beauty, an intriguing mix of the extravagant and restrained but unmistakeably elegant.

◉ Map p28, B6

www.patrimonio
nacional.es

Calle de Bailén

adult/concession €10
guide/audioguide/pa
phlet €7/4/1, EU citiz
free 5-8pm Wed & Th

◷ 10am-8pm

Ⓜ Ópera

Facade of Palacio Real

on't Miss

macia Real

Farmacia Real (Royal Pharmacy), the first set ooms to the right at the southern end of the a de la Armería (Plaza de Armas; Plaza of the oury) courtyard, contains a formidable col- ion of medicine jars and stills for mixing royal coctions; the royals were either paranoid or dedly sickly.

ón del Trono

n the northern end of the Plaza de la ería, the main stairway, a grand statement nperial power, leads to the royal apartments eventually to the Salón del Trono (Throne m). The room is nauseatingly lavish with its nson-velvet wall coverings complemented by a ng painted by the dramatic Venetian baroque ter, Tiepolo, who was a favourite of Carlos III.

parini & Porcelana

se to the Throne Room, the Salón de parini (Gasparini Room) has an exquisite co ceiling and walls resplendent with em- dered silks. The aesthetic may be different he Sala de Porcelana (Porcelain Room), but aura of extravagance continues with myriad es from the one-time Retiro porcelain factory wed into the walls.

dines de Sabatini

French-inspired Jardines de Sabatini lie g the northern flank of the Palacio Real. They e laid out in the 1930s to replace the royal les that once stood on the site.

☑ **Top Tips**

▶ Plan to get here at 10am before the tour buses start to arrive.

▶ A colourful changing of the guard in full parade dress takes place at noon on the first Wednesday of every month (except August and September) between the palace and the cathedral.

▶ A guided tour or audioguide will greatly enhance your experience of the palace.

▶ Don't be surprised if the palace is closed because an official re- ception is taking place.

✖ **Take a Break**

There are few more beautiful vantage points than the outdoor tables at Cafe de Oriente (p34) – perfect for a coffee or wine.

El Café de la Ópera

(☏91 542 63 82; www .elcafedelaopera.com; Calle de Arrieta 6; ⊙8am-mid- night; ⓜÓpera), across the road from Madrid's opera house, the Tea- tro Real has a refined air, wi-fi and live opera in the evenings.

Sights

Plaza de la Villa
SQUARE

1 Map p28, C6

The intimate Plaza de la Villa is enclosed on three sides by fine examples of 17th-century *barroco madrileño* (Madrid-style baroque architecture: a pleasing amalgam of brick, exposed stone and wrought iron). On the western side of the square is the 17th-century former **ayuntamiento** (town hall), in Habsburg-style baroque with Herrerian slate-tile spires. On the opposite side of the square is the Gothic **Casa de los Lujanes**, while the plateresque (15th- and 16th-century Spanish baroque) **Casa de Cisneros**, built in 1537 with later Renaissance alterations, also catches the eye. (Plaza de la Villa; Ⓜ Ópera)

Convento de las Descalzas Reales
CONVENT

2 Map p28, D5

The grim, prisonlike walls of this one-time palace keep modern Madrid at bay and offer no hint that behind the sober plateresque facade lies a sumptuous stronghold of the Catholic faith. The compulsory guided tour (in Spanish) leads you up a gaudily frescoed Renaissance stairway to the upper level of the cloister. You'll also pass through the 33 chapels – a maximum of 33 Franciscan nuns are allowed to live here as part of a closed order – as well as view the antechoir, choir stalls and some of the most extraordinary tapestries you're ever likely to see. (Convent of the Barefoot Royals; www.patrimonionacional.es; Plaza de las Descalzas 3; adult/child €7/4, incl Convento de la Encarnación €10/5, EU citizens free Wed & Thu afternoon; ⏱10.30am-2pm & 4-6.30pm Tue-Sat, 10am-3pm Sun; Ⓜ Ópera, Sol)

Plaza de Oriente
SQUARE

3 Map p28, B5

Watched over by the royal palace, Madrid's opera house and apartments that cost the equivalent of a royal salary, Plaza de Oriente is a living, breathing monument to imperial Madrid. At the centre of the plaza, which the palace overlooks, is an equestrian statue of Felipe IV which was designed by Velázquez, while nearby

---

Top Tip
Cathedral Extras

Climb up through the Museo de la Catedral y Cúpola of the Catedral de Nuestra Señora de la Almudena on the northern facade, opposite the Palacio Real, for fine views from the summit. Down the hill beneath the cathedral's southern wall on Calle Mayor is the neo-Romanesque crypt with more than 400 columns, 20 chapels and fine stained-glass windows.

za de la Villa

some 20 marble statues of mostly ient monarchs. Local legend has at these ageing royals get down heir pedestals at night to stretch r legs. The adjacent **Jardines o Naval** is a great place to watch sun set. (Plaza de Oriente; **M**Ópera)

edral de Nuestra Señora la Almudena   CATHEDRAL

◉ Map p28, B6

exterior of Madrid's cathedral sits armony with the adjacent Palacio l, but its neo-Gothic interior ks the old-world gravitas that so inguishes great cathedrals; begun 879, it wasn't finished until 1992.

(☎91 542 22 00; www.museocatedral .archimadrid.es; Calle de Bailén; cathedral & crypt by donation, museum adult/child €6/4; ⊗9am-8.30pm Mon-Sat, for Mass Sun, museum 10am-2.30pm Mon-Sat; **M**Ópera)

Iglesia de San Ginés   CHURCH

5 ◉ Map p28, D6

San Ginés is one of Madrid's oldest churches: it has been here in one form or another since at least the 14th century. The church houses some fine paintings, including El Greco's *Expulsion of the Moneychangers from the Temple* (1614). (Calle del Arenal 13; ⊗8.45am-1pm & 6-9pm Mon-Sat, 9.45am-2pm & 6-9pm Sun; **M**Sol, Ópera)

Eating

Mercado de San Miguel TAPAS €

6 Map p28, C6

Within the early 20th-century glass walls of one of Madrid's oldest and most beautiful markets, this stunningly renovated spot is an inviting space where you can order tapas and sometimes more substantial plates at most of the counter-bars. When it's full (which is often), the atmosphere is electric. (www.mercadodesanmiguel.es; Plaza de San Miguel; tapas from €1; ☺10am-midnight Sun-Wed, 10am-2am Thu-Sat; ⓂSol)

Restaurante Sobrino de Botín CASTILIAN €€

7 Map p28, D7

Recognised by the *Guinness Book of Records* as the world's oldest restaurant (established in 1725), Sobrino de Botín has appeared in many novels about Madrid (from Ernest Heming-

way to Frederick Forsyth. The secre of its staying power is fine *cochinil* (roast suckling pig; €24) and *corde asado* (roast lamb; €24) cooked in wood-fired ovens. Eating in the vaulted cellar is a treat. (☏91 366 42 17; www.botin.es; Calle de los Cuchilleros 1 mains €18.50-28; ⓂLa Latina, Sol)

Casa Revuelta TAP

8 Map p28, D7

Casa Revuelta puts out some of Madrid's finest tapas of *bacalao* (dried and salted cod; €2.60) bar none. While aficionados of Casa La (p57) may disagree, the fact that th octogenarian owner, Señor Revuelt painstakingly extracts every fish bc in the morning and serves as a wai in the afternoon wins the argumen for us. Early on a Sunday afternoor as the Rastro crowd gathers here, i filled to the rafters. It's also famous for its *callos* (tripe), *torreznos* (bac bits) and *albóndigas* (meatballs). ([. 366 33 32; Calle de Latoneros 3; tapas fror €2.60; ☺10.30am-4pm & 7-11pm Tue-Sat, 10.30am-4pm Sun, closed Aug; ⓂSol, La Latina)

Taberna La Bola MADRILEÑ

9 Map p28, C4

Taberna La Bola (going strong since 1870 and run by the sixth generatio the Verdasco family) is one of the b places in the city to try local Madri cuisine: if you're going to try *cocido a la madrileña* (meat-and-chickpea

☑ Top Tip

Another View

For an alternative slant on the Palacio Real and Plaza de Oriente, head for the Plaza de la Encarnación, immediately northeast of the Jardines Cabo Naval. If the leaves are in full bloom, you won't see much, but otherwise it's a more intimate take through the trees than most views of the palace.

Understand
Madrid & the Spanish Royal Family

When **Felipe II** (r 1556–98) ascended the Spanish throne, Madrid was an obscure provincial outpost, home to just 30,000 people and dwarfed by Toledo, Seville and Valladolid. But Felipe II changed Madrid's fortunes forever in 1561 when he chose the city as Spain's capital and transformed it into the capital of an empire on which the sun never set.

Felipe V (r 1700–46) may have lost most of Spain's European possessions during the Europe-wide War of the Spanish Succession (1702–13), but his reign is notable, not least because he was the first monarch of the Bourbon dynasty; a dynasty that still rules Spain today. His centralisation of state control and attempts at land reform began the process of transforming Spain into a modern European nation, and the former clearly cemented Madrid's claims as Spain's pre-eminent city. Felipe V also laid the plans for the Palacio Real (Royal Palace).

Carlos III (r 1759–88) came to be known as the best 'mayor' Madrid had ever had. He introduced Madrid's first program of sanitation and public hygiene, completed the Palacio Real, inaugurated the Real Jardín Botánico (Royal Botanical Garden) and embarked on a major road-building program. His stamp upon Madrid's essential character was also evident in his sponsorship of local and foreign artists, among them Goya and Tiepolo.

Juan Carlos I (r 1975–) was a protégé of Franco, and the dictator's apparently loyal lieutenant, but Spain's current king would go on to confound his critics by overseeing (some would say engineering) Spain's transition to democracy. When aged just 37, he took the throne two days after Franco died and in July 1976 he appointed Adolfo Suárez, a 43-year-old former Franco apparatchik, as prime minister. To general surprise, and with the king's support, Suárez convinced the Cortes (parliament) to approve a new, two-chamber system. In 1981, the king was once again forced to declare his hand, when a group of armed Guardia Civil led by Lt Col Antonio Tejero attempted a coup by occupying the parliament building. The king appeared on national television to denounce them and the coup collapsed.

stew; €19.50) while in Madrid, this is a good place to do so. It's busy and noisy and very Madrid. (☎91 547 69 30; www .labola.es; Calle de la Bola 5; mains €16-24; ☺lunch & dinner Mon-Sat, lunch Sun, closed Aug; Ⓜ Santo Domingo)

Kitchen Stories   SPANISH €

10 ☒ Map p28, D7

Kitchen Stories, at the foot of the Arco de Cuchilleros stairs off Plaza Mayor's southwestern corner, is a refreshing break from the often classical cooking in the area. It's a bright modern space where Spanish flavours are blended with international tastes. (☎91 366 97 71; www.kitchenstories.es; Calle de los Cuchilleros 3; mains €5.40-16.50; ☺noon-1am; Ⓜ Sol, La Latina)

Bar La Ideal   MADRILEÑO €

11 ☒ Map p28, D7

Spanish bars don't come any more basic than this, but La Ideal is the purveyor of an enduring and wildly popular Madrid tradition – the *boca-dillo de calamares* (a roll stuffed with deep-fried calamari). (☎91 365 72 78; Calle de los Botaderos 4; bocadillos €2.50; ☺lunch & dinner until late; ✷; Ⓜ Sol)

Drinking

Cafe De Oriente   CAFE

12 ☕ Map p28, C5

The outdoor tables of this distinguished old cafe are among the most sought-after in central Madrid,

 Top Tip

Local Specialties

In addition to the chickpea-and-meat hotpot that is *cocido a la madrileña*, Taberna La Bola (p32) serves up other Madrid specialtie. such as *callos* (tripe) and *sopa castellana* (garlic soup).

providing as they do a front-row se for the beautiful Plaza de Oriente, with the Palacio Real as a backdro It's the perfect spot for a coffee wh the weather's fine. (Plaza de Oriente 2; ☺8.30am-1.30am Mon-Thu, 9am-2.30am & Sat, 9am-1.30am Sun; Ⓜ Ópera)

Café del Real   COCKTAIL BAR, (

13 ☕ Map p28, C5

A cafe and cocktail bar in equal pa this intimate little place serves up creative coffees and a few cocktails the soundtrack of chill-out music. best seats are upstairs, where the l ceilings, wooden beams and leathe chairs are a great place to pass an afternoon with friends. (Plaza de Isab II 2; ☺9am-1am Mon-Thu, 9am-3am Fri & ! Ⓜ Ópera)

Chocolatería de San Ginés

14 ☕ Map p28, D6

One of the grand icons of the Mad night, this *chocolate con churros* (Spanish donuts with chocolate) ca sees a sprinkling of tourists throug

the day, but locals usually pack
ut in their search for sustenance
heir way home from a nightclub
etime close to dawn. (Pasadizo de
Ginés 5; ⊙9.30am-7am; Ⓜ Sol)

ticafé CAFE

Ⓠ Map p28, C6

emian kitsch in the best sense
he prevailing theme here and it
s right through the decor, regular
ural events (poetry readings and
certs) and, of course, the clientele.
fees are as popular as the alcohol,
ough that rather strange predilec-
 wears off as the night progresses.
le de la Unión 2; ⊙7pm-2am Mon-Thu,
-2.30am Fri, 5pm-2.30am Sat, 5pm-
night Sun; Ⓜ Ópera)

ntertainment

fé de Chinitas FLAMENCO

Map p28, C4

 of the most distinguished
laos (flamenco venues) in Madrid,
é de Chinitas has an elegant
ing and top-notch flamenco
formers. You can order a meal off
 menu (around €50 per person on
 of the admission price) or simply
 a drink (coffee costs €5!). (☎91
 15 02; www.chinitas.com; Calle de Torija
 dmission incl drink €32; ⊙shows 8pm &
 0pm Mon-Sat; Ⓜ Santo Domingo)

El Berlín Jazz Café JAZZ

17 ⭐ Map p28, D4

El Berlín has been something of a
Madrid jazz stalwart since the 1950s
with headline acts reading like a
who's-who of world jazz. It's all about
classic jazz here and an art deco interior adds to the charm. The headline
acts take to the stage at 11.30pm on
Fridays and Saturdays, with other
performances sprinkled throughout
the week, including a Tuesday jam
session. (☎91 521 57 52; www.cafeberlin.es;
Calle de Jacometrezo 4; admission €8;
⊙7pm-2.30am Tue-Sun Sep-Jul; 👶;
Ⓜ Callao, Santo Domingo)

Las Tablas FLAMENCO

18 ⭐ Map p28, B3

Las Tablas has a reputation for quality
flamenco and reasonable prices. Most
nights you'll see a classic flamenco
show, with plenty of throaty singing
and soul-baring dancing. Antonia
Moya and Marisol Navarro, leading
lights in the flamenco world, are regular performers here. (☎91 542 05 20;
www.lastablasmadrid.com; Plaza de España 9;
admission €26; ⊙shows 10.30pm Sun-Thu,
8pm & 10pm Fri & Sat; Ⓜ Plaza de España)

Teatro Joy Eslava CLUB

19 ⭐ Map p28, D6

This grand old Madrid dance club
(housed in a 19th-century theatre)
claims to have operated every single

Teatro Joy Eslava (p35)

day for the past three decades. Every night's a little different: Loco Monday kicks off the week in spectacular fashion, Thursday is student night and Friday's 'Fabulush' is all about glamour. Throw in occasional live acts and cabaret-style performances on stage and it's a point of reference for Madrid's professional party crowd. (Joy Madrid; ☑91 366 37 33; www.joy-eslava .com; Calle del Arenal 11; admission €12-15; ◷11.30pm-6am; Ⓜ Sol)

Cool
CLUB

20 ⭐ Map p28, C3

One of the hottest clubs in the city, the Philippe Starck–designed curvy white lines, discreet lounge chairs in dark corners and pulsating dance

floor here are accompanied by gorgeous people, gorgeous clothes and strict entry policy. Saturdays draw predominantly gay clientele. Thing don't really get going until 3am. (☑ 733 35 05; www.fsmgroup.es; Calle de Isab Católica 6; admission from €10; ◷midnig 6am Thu-Sat; Ⓜ Santo Domingo)

Teatro Real
OPERA, CLASSICAL M

21 ⭐ Map p28, C5

After spending €100 million-plus a long rebuilding project, the Teat Real is the city's grandest stage for elaborate operas, ballets and class cal music. For the best seats, don't expect change from €127. (☑902 2 48; www.teatro-real.com; Plaza de Oriente Ⓜ Ópera)

hopping

tigua Casa avera

CERAMICS

🔒 Map p28, D4

extraordinary tiled facade of this derful old shop conceals an Alad- s cave of ceramics from all over in. This is not the mass-produced f aimed at a tourist market, but es from the small family potters of alucía and Toledo. (Calle de Isabel la lica 2; ⏰10am-1.30pm & 5-8pm Mon-Fri, n-1.30pm Sat; Ⓜ Santo Domingo)

rco Artesanía

HANDICRAFTS

🔒 Map p28, D7

s original shop in the southwestern er of Plaza Mayor sells an out- ding array of homemade designer venirs, from stone and glass work ewellery and home fittings. The ier mâché figures are gorgeous. w.artesaniaelarco.com; Plaza Mayor 9; am-9pm; Ⓜ Sol, La Latina)

sa Hernanz

SHOES

🔒 Map p28, D7

y've been hand-making the comfy, e-soled *alpargatas* (espadrilles), in's traditional summer footwear, five generations here. Prices range n €5 to €40 and queues form never the weather starts to warm (Calle de Toledo 18; ⏰9am-1.30pm & -8pm Mon-Fri, 10am-2pm Sat; Ⓜ La a, Sol)

El Flamenco Vive

FLAMENCO

25 🔒 Map p28, C6

This temple to flamenco has it all, from guitars and songbooks to well-priced CDs, polka-dotted dancing costumes, shoes, colourful plastic jewellery and literature about flamenco. (www.elflamencovive.es; Calle Conde de Lemos 7; ⏰10.30am-2pm & 5-9pm Mon-Sat; Ⓜ Ópera)

Maty

FLAMENCO

26 🔒 Map p28, E5

Here you'll find flamenco dresses, flamenco shoes and all the accessories that go with the genre, with sizes for children and adults. It also does quality disguises for Carnaval. These are the real deal, with prices to match, but they make brilliant gifts. (✆91 531 32 91; Calle del Maestro Victoria 2; ⏰10am-1.45pm & 4.30-8pm Mon-Fri, 10am-2pm & 4.30-8pm Sat; Ⓜ Sol)

Salvador Bachiller

ACCESSORIES

27 🔒 Map p28, C3

The stylish and high-quality leather bags, wallets, suitcases and other accessories of Salvador Bachiller are a staple of Spanish shopping aficionados. This is leather with a typically Spanish twist – the colours are dazzling in bright pinks, yellows and greens. (www.salvadorbachiller.com; Gran Vía 65; ⏰10am-9.30pm Mon-Sat, 11am-9pm Sun; Ⓜ Plaza de España, Santo Domingo)

Explore

La Latina & Lavapiés

La Latina combines Madrid's best selection of tapas bars and a medieval streetscape studded with elegant churches. Calle de la Cava Baja could just be our favourite street in town for tapas. Multicultural Lavapiés is a world away, at once one of the city's oldest and most traditional *barrios* and home to more immigrants than any other central Madrid *barrio*.

e Sights in a Day

The **Basílica de San Francisco El Grande** (p44) is one Madrid's most imposing churches its many treasures are a fine way to t the day. A walk up the hill through Morería, medieval Madrid's Muslim rter, takes you to lovely Plaza de la a, watched over by the **Iglesia de Andrés** (p44). Enjoy a funky lunch a Musa Latina (p45).

The free **Museo de los Orí-genes** (p44) is one of Madrid's re rewarding museums. Shop for ellery at **Helena Rohner** (p49), then ander down the hill to Lavapiés, niring architectural gems such as La rala, a traditional Madrid tenement ck with communal balconies. A quiet k high above it all at **Gaudeamus é** (p46) is a wonderful way to pass afternoon.

Return up the hill to Calle de la Cava Baja and its surrounding ets. **Taberna Tempranillo** (p47) tures the spirit of the *barrio,* but where along this iconic street is as d for pre-dinner tapas as it is for a k. Follow a flamenco show at **Casa as** (p47) with dinner at **Posada de illa** (p46), then dance the night ay at **ContraClub** (p49).

a local's day in El Rastro and La na, see p40.

Local Life

El Rastro Sunday (p40)

Best of La Latina & Lavapiés

Getting There

M Metro La Latina (line 5) and Lavapiés (line 3) deposit you in the heart of these two *barrios.* Otherwise Tirso de Molina (line 1) and Antón Martín (line 1) on the neighbourhood's northeastern fringe are the only others that are useful.

Local Life
El Rastro Sunday

There are few more enduring Madrid traditions than visiting El Rastro, believed to be Europe's largest flea market, on a Sunday. But El Rastro is so much more than a market, and is instead the prelude to an afternoon of vermouth and tapas in the bars of La Latina. Join the locals, and you'll fulfil a key criteria to being considered a *madrileño*.

❶ El Rastro

You could easily spend a morning inc ing your way down the Calle de la Rib era de Curtidores that hosts **El Rastro** (Ribera de Curtidores; ☺8am-3pm Sun; Ⓜ L Latina) every Sunday morning. Cheap clothes, old flamenco records, even ol photos of Madrid, faux designer purse grungy T-shirts and household goods are the main fare. For every 10 pieces junk, there's a real gem (a lost master piece, an Underwood typewriter...).

Vermouth Hour

…day. One o'clock in the afternoon. …usy bar along Calle de la Cava …a. Welcome to *la hora del vermut* …rmouth hour), a long-standing …drid tradition whereby friends and …ilies enjoy a post-Rastro aperitif . …s tradition is deeply engrained in …*drileño* culture and most such bars … along or just off Calle de la Cava …a.

Txirimiri

…ry local has their favourite place … ordering a *pincho de tortilla* (a …a of *tortilla de patatas*, the quin-…sentially Spanish potato omelette). …t food critics and your average …nter alike are drawn in ever-…reasing numbers to the Basque bar …**rimiri** (91 364 11 96; www.txirimiri.es; …e del Humilladero 6; tapas from €4; …unch & dinner Mon-Sat, closed Aug; M La …na). The tortilla is moist, it's impos-…le to stop at one, and it's utterly …icious.

Almendro 13

…**nendro 13** (91 365 42 52; Calle del …endro 13; mains €7-15; M La Latina) is …ildly popular taberna where you …ne for traditional Spanish tapas …th an emphasis on quality rather …n frilly elaborations. Cured meats, …eses, omelettes and many varia-…ns on these themes dominate the …nu; the famously good *huevos* …os (literally, 'broken eggs') served …th *jamón* and thin potato slices is … star.

5 Casa Lucas

Casa Lucas takes a sideways glance at traditional Spanish tapas, then heads off in new directions. There are a range of hot and cold tapas and larger *raciones*. The menu changes regularly as it comes up with new ideas, and it pays particular attention to its wine list.

6 Taberna de Conspiradores

More than holding its own along-side more illustrious tapas bars, this pokey little bar at the northern end of Calle de la Cava Baja has a confiding air. The food owes everything to the regional cuisine of Extremadura (the *jamón* and other cured meats from there are some of Spain's best), with well-priced wines to wash it down.

7 Plaza de San Andrés

While half of Madrid filters out across the city, either heading home or to the Parque del Buen Retiro, the remainder hang out in the Plaza de San Andrés, with its storeys-high mural and fine church backdrop. As the sun nears the horizon, the light softens and the gathered hordes start the drumbeats and begin to dance.

8 Delic

We could go on for hours about **Delic** (www.delic.es; Costanilla de San Andrés 14; 11am-2am Fri-Sun & Tue-Thu, 7pm-2am Mon; M La Latina), a long-standing cafe-bar, but simply put: nursing an exceptional-ly good mojito (€8) or three on a warm summer's evening at Delic's outdoor tables on one of Madrid's prettiest plazas is one of life's great pleasures. Bliss.

Parque
de Atenas

A

B

C

D

Parque del Eimr
Mohamed I

1

Viaduct

C del Rollo

Plaza
del
Cordón

C de San Justo

C de la Pasa

Plaza del
Conde de
Barajas

Plaza
de Puerta
Cerrada

C del Conde

Plaza del
Alamillo

Jardín
del Príncipe
Anglona

C del Príncipe
Anglona

C de Segovia

19 🄐

Jardines de
las Vistillas

C de la Morería

C de Alfonso VI

Plaza
de la
Paja

Costanilla de
San Pedro

✕14

C del Nuncio

20 🄐

✕ 12 Basílic
Nuestra Se
del Buen Co

18
🌟

Plaza
de Granado

Plaza de
Gabriel
Miró

C de Yeseros

C de Redondilla

✕
6

Museo
de Los
Orígenes

C del Almendro

11 ✕ 9 🄐

C de Grafal de

✕ 7

2

C de la Morería

C de Bailén

Iglesia de
San Andrés

3
●

● 4

16
✕

C de la Cava Baja

C de Toledo

C de Don Pedro

Plaza de
San Andrés

C de la Cava Alta

✕ 5

🄐 21

Plaza de la Puerta
de Moros

Plaza del
Humilladero

C de San M

La Latin Ⓜ

Plaza de
San
Francisco

C de San Isidro Labrador

Carrera de San Francisco

✕
8

Plaza de la Cebada

Pla
Ca.

C de San Buenaventura

C de las Aguas

C de Oriente

C de Humilladero

C de la Cebada

La Latina Ⓜ

3

Basílica de
San Francisco
El Grande

1
●

LA LATINA

C de Luciente

C de Ruda

✕10

C del Ángel

C del Mediodia Grande

C de Toledo

C de Santa Ana

C del Rosario

C de Calatrava

C del Mediodia
Chica

C de las Amazonas

EL RA

Plaza General
Vara del Rey

4

C de la Paloma

C de Toledo

El
Rastro

C de la Ventosa

Gran Vía de San Francisco

C Mira el Río Alta

C del Carnero

C de Carlos Arniches

C de Capitan
San Martinez

C Arganzuela

C Mira el Río Baja

5

Glorieta de
Puerta de
Toledo

Puerta de
Toledo Ⓜ

Plaza
Campillo del
Mundo Nuevo

Ronda de Toledo

E

C de Atocha

F

Plaza de
Jacinto
Benavente

G

N 0 — 200 m
0 — 0.1 miles

H

1

ncepción Jerónima

C de las Huertas

HUERTAS

Plaza de
Matute

Colegiada

C del Conde
de Romanones

C del Doctor Cortezo

C de los Relatores

C de Luiz Vélez
de Guevara

C de Cañízares

17

C de León

M

**Antón
Martín**

**Tirso
de Molina**

Plaza de
Tirso de
Molina

Tirso de Molina

C de la Magdalena

Plaza
de Antón
Martín

M

2

e de Alba Plaza de Tirso de Molina

C de la Espada

C Soler y González

C de Cabeza

C del Ave María

C de la Torrecilla del Leal

Juanelo

C del Calvario

C del Olmo

Encomienda

C de Jesús y María

C de Ministriles

C del Olivar

C Tres Peces

3

s dos Hermanas

C de San Carlos

C de la Esperanza

C de Abades

LAVAPIÉS

C del Oso

C de Cabesteros

C de Mesón de Paredes

C de Lavapiés

C del Ave María

C de Primavera

C de Buena Vista

C de Zurita

C de Salitre

nzález

C de los Embajadores

C del Amparo

Plaza de
Lavapiés

C de la Fé

4

e Rodas

C del Sombrete

M **Lavapiés**

C de Argumosa

a de la Huerta del Bayo

C de Santiago Verde

C de Tribulete

15

C de la Sombrería

l Sol

C de Ventorrito

13

C de Espino

C de Miguel Servet

C de Valencia

C del Doctor Fourquet

5

sino

C Provisiones

Sights

Basílica de San Francisco El Grande
CHURCH

1 Map p42, A3

Lording it over the southwestern corner of La Latina, this baroque basilica has an extravagantly frescoed dome that is, by some estimates, the fourth largest in the world. Highlights include the neo-plateresque Capilla de San Bernardino (where the central fresco was painted by a young Goya), the museum (with works of art by Francisco Zurbarán and Francisco Pacheco, the father-in-law and teacher of Velázquez) and the fine Renaissance *sillería* (sculpted walnut seats) in the sacristy. (Plaza de San Francisco 1; adult/concession €3/2; ⏱mass 8am-10.30am Mon-Sat, museum 10.30am-12.30pm & 4-6pm Tue-Sun; Ⓜ La Latina, Puerta de Toledo)

✅ Top Tip

San Francisco El Grande

Although entry to the Basílica de San Francisco El Grande is free during morning Mass times, there is no access to the museum and the lights in the Capilla de San Bernardino won't be on to illuminate the Goya.

Basílica de Nuestra Señora del Buen Consejo
CHU

2 Map p42, D2

This austere baroque basilica was founded in the 17th century as the headquarters for the Jesuits and is today home to the remains of the city's main patron saint, San Isidro the third chapel on your left after y walk in). (Calle de Toledo 37; ⏱8am-1pm 6-9pm; Ⓜ Tirso de Molina, La Latina)

Iglesia de San Andrés
CHU

3 Map p42, B2

This proud church boasts stern, dark columns with gold-leaf capital against the rear wall that lead your eyes up into the dome, all rose, yell and green, and rich with sculpted fl ral fantasies and cherubs poking ou of every nook and cranny. (Plaza de S Andrés; ⏱8am-1pm & 6-8pm; Ⓜ La Latina

Museo de Los Orígenes
MUSE

4 Map p42, C2

For an overview of Madrid's history, this place is hard to beat, with archaeological finds from the Roma period, maps, scale models, painting and photos of Madrid down throug the ages. (Casa de San Isidro; ☎91 366 74 15; www.madrid.es; Plaza de San Andrés 2; admission free; ⏱9.30am-8pm Tue-Fri, 10am-2pm Sat & Sun Sep-Jul, 9.30am-2.30 Tue-Sat Aug; Ⓜ La Latina)

Top Tip

Capilla del Obispo

round the back of Iglesia de San
ndrés, on Plaza de la Paja, is
e recently restored Capilla del
bispo. Visit from Tuesday to Friday
: 12.30pm for the sung service
ficio del Mediodía'.

ating

berna Matritum TAPAS €€

 Map p42, C2

s little gem is reason enough to
our from the more popular Calle de
Cava Baja next door. The seasonal
nu here encompasses terrific tapas,
ads and generally creative cooking,
l some of the desserts come from
master Catalan chocolatier Oriol
aguer. (☑91 365 82 37; Calle de la Cava
17; mains €13-18; ☺lunch & dinner Wed-
, dinner Mon & Tue; MLa Latina)

Musa
tina CONTEMPORARY SPANISH €€

 Map p42, B2

d-back La Musa Latina has an
r-popular dining area and food
t's designed to bring a smile to
r face – the hanging kebabs have
ieved something close to legendary
tus. The outdoor tables are lovely
en the weather's warm. (☑91 354
55; www.lamusalatina.com; Costanilla de
Andrés 1; mains €4.50-11.50; ☺lunch &
ner; MLa Latina)

Casa Lucio SPANISH €€

7 Map p42, C2

Lucio has been wowing *madrileños*
with his light touch, quality ingre-
dients and home-style local cooking
for ages – think roasted meats and, a
Lucio speciality, eggs in abundance.
The lunchtime *guisos del día* (stews of
the day), including *cocido* (meat-and-
chickpea stew) on Wednesdays, are
also popular. Dress nicely. (☑91 365 32
52; www.casalucio.es; Calle de la Cava Baja
35; mains €12-25; ☺lunch & dinner Sun-Fri,
dinner Sat, closed Aug; MLa Latina)

Juana La Loca TAPAS €€

8 ✗ Map p42, B3

Juana La Loca does a range of creative
tapas with tempting options lined up
along the bar and more on the menu
that they prepare to order. But we love
it above all for its *tortilla de patatas*
(€4 per *tapa*), which is distinguished
from others of its kind by the caramel-
ised onions – simply wonderful. (☑91
364 05 25; Plaza de la Puerta de Moros 4;
tapas from €4, mains €8-19; ☺lunch & dinner
Tue-Sun, dinner Mon; MLa Latina)

Restaurante Julián
de Tolosa NAVARRAN €€€

9 ✗ Map p42, C2

Navarran cuisine is treated with re-
spect at this classy place that's popular with celebrities and well-regarded
by food critics. There are only four
main dishes to choose from – two
fish and two meat – and they haven't

changed in years. But it still has a contemporary feel and why change the *chuletón* (T-bone steak) when it's already close to perfection. (☎91 365 82 10; www.casajuliandetolosa.com; Calle de la Cava Baja 18; mains €21.50-29.50; ☺lunch & dinner Tue-Sun, lunch Mon; Ⓜ La Latina)

Malacatín
MADRILEÑO €€

 10 Map p42, D3

If you want to see *madrileños* enjoying their favourite local food, this is one of the best places to do so. The clamour of conversation bounces off the tiled walls of the cramped dining area adorned with bullfighting memorabilia. The speciality is as much *cocido* as you can eat (€19). The *degustación de cocido* (taste of stew; €5) at the bar is a great way to try Madrid's favourite dish without going all the way. (☎91 365 52 41; www .malacatin.com; Calle de Ruda 5; mains €11-15; ☺lunch Mon-Wed & Sat, lunch & dinner Thu & Fri; Ⓜ La Latina)

Txacolina
TAPAS €

11 Map p42, C2

If ordering tapas makes you nervous because you don't speak Spanish or you're not quite sure how it works, it couldn't be easier here – they're lined up on the bar, Basque style, in all their glory and you can simply point. Whatever you order, wash it down with a *txacoli*, a sharp Basque white wine. (☎91 366 48 77; Calle de la Cava Baja 26; tapas from €3; ☺dinner Mon & Wed-Fri, lunch & dinner Sat, lunch Sun; Ⓜ La Latina)

Posada de la Villa
MADRILEÑO ●

12 Map p42, D2

This wonderfully restored 17th-cent *posada* (inn) is something of a local landmark. The atmosphere is forma the decoration sombre and traditio (heavy timber and brickwork), and cuisine decidedly local – roast meat *cocido*, *callos* (tripe) and *sopa de aj* (garlic soup). (☎91 366 18 80; www.pos dadelavilla.com; Calle de la Cava Baja 9; ma €20-28; ☺lunch & dinner Mon-Sat, lunch S closed Aug; Ⓜ La Latina)

Drinking

Gaudeamus Café
C

13 Map p42, F5

With a large terrace with views ove the Lavapiés rooftops, it almost seems incidental that it also serves great teas, coffees and snacks (and meals). (www.gaudeamuscafe.com; Calle Tribulete 14, 4th fl; ☺3pm-midnight Mon-S Ⓜ Lavapiés)

Café del Nuncio
BAR, C

 14 Map p42, C1

Café del Nuncio straggles down a laneway to Calle de Segovia. You ca drink on one of several cosy levels inside or, better still in summer, enj the outdoor seating that one local reviewer likened to a slice of Rome. (Calle de Segovia 9; ☺noon-2am Sun-Thu, noon-3am Fri & Sat; Ⓜ La Latina)

Eucalipto   COCKTAIL BAR

Map p42, G4

'd be mad to at least pass by
s fine little bar with its love of all
ngs Cuban. From the music to the
ntele and the Caribbean cocktails
cluding nonalcoholic), it's a sexy,
d-back place. Not surprisingly, the
jitos are a cut above average. (Calle
rgumosa 4; ☉5pm-2am Sun-Thu, 5pm-
h Fri & Sat; ⓂLavapiés)

berna Tempranillo   WINE BAR

Map p42, C2

could come here for the tapas, but
recommend Taberna Tempranillo
marily for its wines, of which it has

a selection that puts many Spanish
bars to shame, and many are sold
by the glass. (Calle de la Cava Baja 38;
☉1-3.30pm & 8pm-midnight Tue-Sun, 8pm-
midnight Mon; ⓂLa Latina)

Entertainment

Casa Patas   FLAMENCO

17 ⭐ Map p42, G2

One of the top flamenco stages in
Madrid, this *tablao* (restaurant with
a flamenco floorshow) always offers
flawless quality that serves as a good
introduction to the art. It's not the
friendliest place in town, but no one
complains about the standard of the

asa Patas

Understand

Tapas: A Primer

- -

Many would argue that tapas are Spain's greatest culinary gift to the world. While devotees of paella and *jamón* can make a convincing counterclaim, what clinches it for us is the fact that the potential variety for tapas is endless.

Anything can be a *tapa* (a single item of tapas), from a handful of olives or a slice of *jamón* on bread to a *tortilla de patatas* (Spanish potato omelette) served in liquefied form. That's because tapas is the canvas upon which Spanish chefs paint the story of a nation's obsession with food, the means by which they show their fidelity to traditional Spanish tastes even as they gently nudge their compatriots in never-before-imagined directions. By making the most of very little, tapas serves as a link to the impoverished Madrid of centuries past. By re-imagining even the most sacred Spanish staples, tapas is the culinary trademark of a confident country rushing headlong into the future.

Tapas Etiquette

To many visitors, ordering tapas can seem one of the dark arts of Spanish etiquette. Fear not: in many bars in Madrid, it couldn't be easier. With so many tapas varieties lined up along the bar, you either take a small plate and help yourself or point to the morsel you want. In such cases, it's customary to keep track of what you eat (by holding on to the toothpicks for example) and then tell the bar staff how many you've had when it's time to pay. Otherwise, many places have a list of tapas, either on a menu or posted up behind the bar. If you can't choose, ask for '*la especialidad de la casa*' (the house specialty) and it's hard to go wrong. Another way of eating tapas is to order *raciones* (literally 'rations'; large tapas servings) or *media raciones* (half-rations; smaller tapas servings). These plates and half-plates of a particular dish are a good way to go if you particularly like something and want more than a mere *tapa*. Remember, however, that after a couple of *raciones* most people are almost certainly full.

rmances. (📞91 369 04 96; www.casa
.com; Calle de Cañizares 10; admission
🕐shows 10.30pm Mon-Thu, 9pm &
ight Fri & Sat; Ⓜ Antón Martín, Tirso de
a)

traClub
LIVE MUSIC

 Map p42, A2

raClub is a crossover live music
e and nightclub. After the live acts
thing from flamenco and jazz to
), the resident DJs serve up equally
ctic beats to make sure you don't
e elsewhere. (📞91 365 55 45; www
raclub.es; Calle de Bailén 16; admission
2; 🕐10pm-6am Wed-Sat; Ⓜ La Latina)

hopping

Hierro
CLOTHING, ACCESSORIES

🔒 Map p42, D1

s small boutique has an exceptional
tion of handbags from design-
such as Iñaki Sampedro, Quique
tre and Carlos de Caz. The look is
histicated but colourful. (📞91 364
l; Calle de la Cava Baja 6; 🕐11am-2.30pm
)pm Mon-Sat, noon-3pm Sun; Ⓜ La Latina,
de Molina)

lena Rohner
JEWELLERY

🔒 Map p42, C2

of Europe's most creative jewel-
designers, Helena Rohner has
acious boutique in La Latina.
king with silver, stone, porcelain,
d and Murano glass, she makes

Caramelos Paco

inventive pieces and her work is a
regular feature of Paris fashion shows.
(www.helenarohner.com.es; Calle del Almendro
4; 🕐9am-8.30pm Mon-Fri, noon-2.30pm &
3.30-8pm Sat, noon-3pm Sun; Ⓜ La Latina,
Tirso de Molina)

Caramelos Paco
FOOD

21 🔒 Map p42, D2

A sweet shop that needs to be seen to
be believed, Caramelos Paco has been
indulging children and adults alike
since 1934 and it remains unrivalled
when it comes to variety. (📞91 365
42 58; www.caramelospaco.com; Calle de
Toledo 53-55; 🕐9.30am-2pm & 5-8.30pm
Mon-Fri, 9.30am-2pm Sat, 11am-3pm Sun;
Ⓜ La Latina)

Explore

Sol, Santa Ana & Huertas

The downtown streets around the Plaza de la Puerta del Sol are the sum total of all Madrid's personalities, and it's here that the world *madrileños* most often intersects with that of visitors. Away to the southeast, Plaza de Santa Ana and Huertas combine a stately charm with terrific restaurants and nightlife whose noise reverberates out across the city.

e Sights in a Day

Start your day in Plaza de Santa Ana, one of the city's liveliest most agreeable squares. Spend an r or two wandering the **Barrio de Letras** (p55), then take in the **Real demia de Bellas Artes de San nando** (p55), one of Madrid's most errated art galleries. For lunch, try **Finca de Susana** (p57).

Try and track down the trail of Cervantes in the Barrio de las ras, pause for designer tapas at **Vi ol** (p56), and indulge yourself with umptuous Arab bath at **Hammam Andalus** (p55).

Begin this rather long evening with a sherry at wonderful **La encia** (p58), before embarking on pas crawl via **Casa Alberto** (p56) **Los Gatos** (p57). Consider Ma- d's home of live jazz, **Café Central** 0), or a flamenco show at **Villa sa** (p60). Whichever you choose, ow it up with a cocktail or two at **mperfecto** (p59). Aesthetes will oy the cool rooftop sophistication **a Terraza del Urban** (p59).

a local's night out in Huertas, see 2.

Local Life
A Night Out in Huertas (p52)

Best of Sol, Santa Ana & Huertas

Eating
Casa Alberto (p56)
Vi Cool (p56)
Lhardy (p56)
Los Gatos (p57)
La Terraza del Casino (p57)

Bars
La Venencia (p58)
El Imperfecto (p59)
La Terraza del Urban (p59)
The Penthouse (p53)
Taberna Alhambra (p59)

Live Music
Café Central (p60)
Villa Rosa (p60)
Costello Café & Niteclub (p61)
Sala El Sol (p60)
Cardamomo (p61)

Getting There

Ⓜ **Metro** Sol station (1, 2 & 3) is the most convenient, followed by Sevilla (line 2), Gran Vía (line 1 & 5), Antón Martín (line 1), Banco de España (line 2) and Atocha (line 1).

Local Life
A Night Out in Huertas

As sunset nears, locals begin arriving in the Plaza de Santa Ana and the streets towards Sol and down towards the Paseo del Prado. That's because bars here range from cool and classy rooftop perches to ancient *barrio* classics that haven't changed in decades, plus what is arguably Madrid's finest collection of live-music venues thrown in for good measure.

❶ Taberna de Dolores

Old bottles and beer mugs line the shelves at this Madrid institution. T thirty-something crowd often inclu the odd *famoso* (celebrity) or two. **Taberna de Dolores** (☎91 429 22 43; Plaza de Jesús 4; ⊘11am-1am Sun-Thu, 11a 2am Fri & Sat; Ⓜ Antón Martín) claims to be 'the most famous bar in Madrid' that's pushing it, but it's invariably so who are we to argue?

Maceiras

to surviving long Madrid nights is
r to drink on an empty stomach,
the Galician tapas here (think
pus, green peppers) in **Maceiras**
1 429 15 84; Calle de las Huertas 66; mains
; **M** Antón Martín), a rustic bar down
Huertas hill, are outstanding. Wash
wn with a crisp white Ribeiro and
re halfway to being a local.

Jazz Bar

jazz aficionados begin the night
azz Bar (91 429 70 31; www.jazzbar
Calle de Moratín 35; 3pm-2.30am;
tón Martín) before heading onto
performances elsewhere. With
ndless jazz soundtrack, discreet
er booths and plenty of greenery,
ot surprising that many return
r in the night.

Populart

ulart (91 429 84 07; www.populart
alle de las Huertas 22; admission free;
m-2.30am Sun-Thu, 6pm-3.30am Fri &
M Antón Martín, Sol) offers a low-key
osphere and top-quality music,
h is mostly jazz with occasional
s, swing and even flamenco
wn into the mix. Compay Seg-
, Sonny Fortune and the Canal
et Jazz Band have all played here.
ws start at 10.45pm.

Casa Pueblo

oried Huertas bar that prides itself
ree live jazz and a bohemian out-
, **Casa Pueblo** (91 420 20 38; Calle
ón 3; 9pm-2am Tue-Sun; **M** Antón

Martín or Banco de España) is an agreeable
bar serving up a winning combination
of cakes and cocktails, and draws an
in-the-know thirty-something crowd.

❻ La Boca del Lobo

La Boca del Lobo (91 429 70 13; www
.labocadellobo.com; Calle de Echegaray 11;
admission free-€10; 9pm-3.30am; **M** Sol,
Sevilla) (The Wolf's Mouth) is as dark
as its name suggest and has broadened its horizons from rock to include
just about anything – roots, reggae,
jazz, soul, ska, flamenco, funk and
fusion. Concerts start between 9.30pm
and 11pm Wednesday to Saturday.

❼ The Penthouse

High above the Plaza de Santa Ana,
The Penthouse (91 701 60 20; www.the
penthouse.es; Plaza de Santa Ana 14; admission
€25; 9pm-3am Wed & Thu, 9pm-3.30am
Fri & Sat; **M** Antón Martín, Sol), a sybaritic
open-air (7th-floor) cocktail bar, has
terrific views over Madrid's rooftops.
It's a place for sophisticates, with chill-
out areas with cushions, funky DJs
and a dress policy designed to sort
out the classy from the wannabes.

❽ Stella

Stella (91 531 63 78; www.web-mondo
.com; Calle de Arlabán 7; admission €12;
 12.30-6am Thu-Sat; **M** Sevilla) is one of
the enduring success stories of the
Madrid night, spinning house and
electronica for an appreciative local
audience. The great visuals will leave
you cross-eyed if you weren't already
from the music in this heady place.

Plaza de Santa María Soledad

C del Desengaño

C del Barco

C del Valverde

C del Fuencarral

C de Hortaleza

Plaza de Vásquez de Mella

C de Clavel

C de las Infantas

C de la Libertad

Gran Vía

C de la Salud

C de las Tres Cruces

Gran Vía

Plaza de la Red de San Luis

C del Caballero de Gracia

C de la Reina

Gran Vía

Banco de España

C del Marqués de Valdeiglesias

C de la Abada

C de la Chinchilla

Plaza del Carmen

C de San Alberto

C de la Montera

C de Tetuán

C de la Virgen de los Peligros

Sevilla

C de Casa Riera

C del Carmen

C de Preciados

C Galdo

CENTRO

C de la Aduana

C de Alcalá

Real Academia de Bellas Artes de San Fernando **2**

9

Sevilla

C de los Cedaceros

C de los Madrazo

23

Plaza de la Puerta del Sol

10

1

Sol

Plaza de Canalejas

C de Sevilla

C de Arlabán

12

C de Zorrilla

C del Arenal

28 Carrera de San Jerónimo

C Mayor

C del Correo

C de la Paz

C de las Carretas

21

30

C de Espoz y Mina

18

C de la Victoria

7

C del Pozo

C de la Cruz

31

C de Echegaray

15

17

Carrera de San Je

Plaza de las Cortes

19

SOL

C del Príncipe

27

C de Ventura de la Vega

29

C de la Bolsa

Hammam al-Andalus

4

Plaza de Jacinto Benavente

22

C de Barcelona

13

Callejón de Álvarez Gato

25

Plaza del Ángel

Plaza de Santa Ana

11

C de Manuel Fernández y González

32

C de Manuel

C del Prado

C de San Agustín

3

Barr de la Letr

C de la Concepción Jerónima

C del Doctor Cortezo

C de los Relatores

C de Luis Vélez de Guevara

C de San Sebastián

6

5

Plaza de Matute

16

C de León

HUERTAS

14

C de Lope de

C de Cervante

C Quevedo

C de las Huertas

20

C de Santa María

C del Conde de Romanones

C del Olivar

C de Atocha

C del Ave María

Antón Martín

C del Amor de Dios

Plaza de Antón Martín

C de Moratín

C de la Magdalena

C de Cabeza

C de Santa Isabel

Antón Martín

C del Olmo

LAVAPIÉS

For reviews see		
◎ Sights	p55
✕ Eating	p56
◑ Drinking	p58
✪ Entertainment	p60
🔒 Shopping	p61

0 0.1

ghts

za de la
erta del Sol
SQUARE

 Map p54, A3

drid's true downtown, the Puerta
Sol is a graceful hemisphere of
ant facades and often overwhelm-
crowds. The main building on the
are, the Casa de Correos, was built
he city's main post office in 1768.
east of Carlos III's statue, the
ue of a bear nuzzling a *madroño*
awberry tree) is the city's symbol.
za de la Puerta del Sol; **M** Sol)

al Academia de Bellas
es de San Fernando
MUSEUM

 Map p54, B2

entre for artistic excellence since
nando VI founded it in the 18th
tury (both Picasso and Dalí stud-
here), it houses works by some of
best-loved old masters. Highlights
ude works by Zurbarán, El Greco,
ens, Tintoretto, Goya, Sorolla and
n Gris, not to mention a couple of
or portraits by Velázquez and a
drawings by Picasso. (☎ 91 524 08
http://rabasf.insde.es; Calle de Alcalá 13;
t/child €5/free, free Wed; ⊙ 9am-3pm
Sat, 9am-2.30pm Sun Sep-Jun, hours
Jul & Aug; **M** Sol, Sevilla)

Barrio de
las Letras
NEIGHBOURHOOD

3 Map p54, D4

The area that unfurls down the hill
east of Plaza de Santa Ana is referred
to as the *Barrio de las Letras* (District
of Letters). Miguel de Cervantes
Saavedra (1547–1616), the author of
Don Quijote, lived and died at **Calle
de Cervantes 2**. He is thought to
be buried around the corner at the
Convento de las Trinitarias (Calle de
Lope de Vega 16; **M** Antón Martín), which is
marked by another plaque. Another
literary landmark is the **Casa de
Lope de Vega** (☎ 91 429 92 16; Calle de
Cervantes 11; admission free; ⊙ guided tours
every 30min 10am-2pm Tue-Sat; **M** Antón
Martín), the former home of Lope de
Vega (1562–1635), Spain's premier
playwright. (**M** Antón Martín)

Hammam al-Andalus
DAY SPA

4 Map p54, A4

Hammam al-Andalus is both an
architectural jewel and a sensory indulgence that takes you back in time.

 Top Tip

It's Free

The Real Academia de Bellas Artes
de San Fernando may have a collection the envy of many a European gallery but it's free to enjoy if
you come on a Wednesday.

Top Tip

Cheap Baths

Prices at Hammam al-Andalus, Madrid's best Arab bath, are cheapest from 10am to 4pm Monday to Friday (from €24 for the basic bath experience); otherwise, you'll pay from €27.50 up to €76.50 for the full bath and massages experience, depending on the package; there are discounts for students and for those over 65.

Housed in the excavated cellars of old Madrid, this imitation traditional Arab bath offers massages and aromatherapy beneath graceful arches, accompanied by the sound of trickling water. Reservations are required. (http://madrid.hammamalandalus.com; Calle de Atocha 14; treatments €24-76.50; ⊘10am-midnight; Ⓜ Sol)

Eating

Casa Alberto
SPANISH €€

 5 Map p54, C4

One of the most atmospheric old *tabernas* (taverns) of Madrid, Casa Alberto has been around since 1827. The secret to its staying power is vermouth on tap, excellent tapas at the bar and fine sit-down meals; Casa Alberto's *rabo de toro* (bull's tail) is famous among aficionados. *Jamón*,

Manchego cheese and *croquetas* are recurring themes. (☑91 429 93 56; www .casalberto.es; Calle de las Huertas 18; mains €16-20; ⊘lunch & dinner Tue-Sat, lunch S Ⓜ Antón Martín)

Vi Cool
CONTEMPORARY SPANISH

 6 Map p54, B4

Catalan master chef Sergi Arola is of the most creative culinary talent in the country. This modern bar-st space with reasonable prices enabl average mortals to sample Arola's formidable gastronomic skills. Dish are either tapas or larger *raciones*. (☑91 429 49 13; www.vi-cool.com; Calle d las Huertas 12; mains €8-18; ⊘lunch & di daily; Ⓜ Antón Martín)

Lhardy
MADRILEÑO

 7 Map p54, B3

This Madrid landmark (since 1839 an elegant treasure trove of takeaw gourmet tapas downstairs, while the six upstairs dining areas are th upmarket preserve of traditional Madrid dishes with an occasional of French influence. House specialities include *cocido a la madrileñ* (meat-and-chickpea stew; €35.50) pheasant and wild duck in an oran perfume. (☑91 521 33 85; www.lhardy.c Carrera de San Jerónimo 8; mains €18.50-⊘lunch & dinner Mon-Sat, lunch Sun, clos Aug; Ⓜ Sol, Sevilla)

Gatos
TAPAS €€

 Map p54, D4

..s you can point to without
..phering the menu and eclectic
world decor make this a popular
..ce down the bottom end of Huer-
.. The most popular orders are the
..apés (tapas on toast), which, we
.. to say, are rather delicious. (☎91
..30 67; Calle de Jesús 2; tapas from €3.50;
..on-1am Sun-Thu, noon-2am Fri & Sat;
..ntón Martín)

Terraza del
..sino
CONTEMPORARY SPANISH €€€

 Map p54, C2

..ched atop the landmark Casino
..Madrid building, this temple of
..te cuisine is overseen, albeit from
.., by Ferran Adrià (Spain's premier
..brity chef), but is mostly in the
..ds of his acolyte Paco Roncero. It's
..bout culinary experimentation,
.. a menu that changes as each new
.. emerges from the laboratory and
.. the kitchen. (☎91 521 87 00; www
..nodemadrid.es; Calle de Alcalá 15; set
..us from €100; ☉lunch & dinner Mon-Fri,
..er Sat; Ⓜ Sevilla)

..sa Labra
TAPAS €

 Map p54, A3

..a Labra has been going strong
.. e 1860, an era that the decor
..ngly evokes. Locals love their
..alao (cod) and ordering it here –
..er as deep-fried tapas (una tajada
..acalao goes for €1.25) or as una

croqueta de bacalao (€0.80 per cro-
quette) – is a Madrid rite of initiation.
It's the sort of place that fathers bring
their sons, just as their fathers did
before them. (☎91 532 14 05; www.casa
labra.es; Calle de Tetuán 11; tapas from €1;
☉9.30am-3.30pm & 5.30-11pm; Ⓜ Sol)

El Lateral
TAPAS €

11 Map p54, B4

Our pick of the bars surrounding
Plaza de Santa Ana, El Lateral does
terrific *pinchos* (tapas), the perfect
accompaniment to the fine wines on
offer. At around €3.50 per pincho,
you could easily pass an evening here
savouring every bite. (☎91 420 15 82;
www.cadenalateral.es; Plaza de Santa Ana
12; pinchos €3.50; ☉noon-1am; Ⓜ Antón
Martín, Sol)

La Finca de Susana
SPANISH €€

12 Map p54, C3

It's difficult to find a better combination of price, quality cooking
and classy atmosphere anywhere in
Huertas. The softly lit dining area is
bathed in greenery and the sometimes
innovative, sometimes traditional food
draws a hip young crowd. No reservations. (www.lafinca-restaurant.com; Calle de
Arlabán 4; mains €7-12; Ⓜ Sevilla)

Las Bravas
TAPAS €

13 Map p54, B4

Las Bravas has long been the place for
a *caña* (small glass of beer) and the
best *patatas bravas* (fried potatoes

A selection of tapas dishes

with a spicy tomato sauce; €3.50) in town. In fact, its version of the *bravas* sauce is so famous that they patented it. (☎91 522 85 81; Callejón de Álvarez Gato 3; raciones €3.50-10; ☺lunch & dinner; Ⓜ Sol, Sevilla)

Sidrería Vasca Zeraín
BASQUE €€

14 ✖ Map p54, D4

In the heart of the Barrio de las Letras, this sophisticated Basque restaurant is one of the best places in town to sample Basque cuisine. The essential staples include cider, *bacalao* and wonderful steaks. We highly recommend the *menú sidrería*

(cider-house menu; €38). (☎91 429 09; www.restaurante-vasco-zerain-sidreria .es; Calle Quevedo 3; mains €14-32; ☺lur & dinner Mon-Sat, lunch Sun, closed Aug; Ⓜ Antón Martín)

Drinking
La Venencia

15 🍺 Map p54, C3

La Venencia is a *barrio* classic, with fine sherry from Sanlúcar and manzanilla from Jeréz all poured straight from the dusty wooden barrels, accompanied by a small selec of tapas with an Andalucian bent.

erwise, there's no music, no flashy ›rations; it's all about you, your (sherry) and your friends. (Calle de garay 7; ⌚1-3.30pm & 7.30pm-1.30am; ›l)

›mperfecto
BAR, LIVE MUSIC

Map p54, C4

ıame notwithstanding, the ›erfect One' is our ideal Huertas with live jazz most Tuesdays at ı and a drinks menu as long as xophone, ranging from cocktails ı and spirits to milkshakes, teas creative coffees. (Plaza de Matute 2; ›m-2am Mon-Thu, 3pm-2.30am Fri & Sat; ıtón Martín)

Terraza del ›an
COCKTAIL BAR

Map p54, C3

; indulgent terrace sits atop the ·star Hotel Urban and has five-star ›s with five-star prices. Worth ·y euro. In case you get vertigo, d downstairs to the similarly high-s **Glass Bar** (⌚11pm-3am). (☎91 787 ›; Carrera de San Jerónimo 34; ⌚10pm-; M Sevilla)

›erna Alhambra
BAR

Map p54, B3

re can be a certain sameness about bars between Sol and Santa Ana, ›h is why this fine old *taberna* stands out. The striking facade and exquisite tile work of the interior are quite beautiful, and the feel is cool, casual and busy. They serve tapas and, later at night, there are some fine flamenco tunes. (www.tabernaalhambra.es; Calle de la Victoria 9; ⌚11am-1.30am Sun-Wed, 11am-2am Thu, 11am-2.30am Fri & Sat; M Sol)

Café del Soul
BAR

19 Map p54, B3

Cocktails (alcoholic €7, nonalcoholic €4.50) are a big selling point these days in Madrid. If you add chill-out music (that turns to chill-house later in the night) and curious decor that incorporates Moroccan lamps, Café del Soul is more mellow than many in the area. (☎91 523 16 06; www.cafedelsoul.es; Calle de Espoz y Mina 14; ⌚4pm-2am Mon-Fri, noon-3am Sat, noon-2am Sun; M Sol)

Dos Gardenias
BAR

20 Map p54, D4

When Huertas starts to overwhelm, this tranquil little bar is the perfect antidote. The flamenco and chill-out music ensure a relaxed vibe, while sofas, softly lit colours and some of the best mojitos (and exotic teas) in the *barrio* make this the perfect spot to ease yourself into or out of the night. (Calle de Santa María 13; ⌚8pm-2.30am Mon-Sat, 5pm-2.30am Sun; M Antón Martín)

Malaspina   BAR

21 Map p54, B3

Although it serves inviting tapas, we like this cosy bar, with its wooden tables and semirustic decor, as a mellow place for a quiet drink before you head home for an early night. (☏91 523 40 24; Calle de Cádiz 9; ☺11am-2am Sun-Thu, 11am-2.30am Fri & Sat; 🛜; Ⓜ Sol)

Entertainment

Café Central   JAZZ

22 ⭐ Map p54, B4

In 2011, the respected jazz magazine *Down Beat* included this art deco bar on the list of the world's best jazz clubs. With well over 9000 gigs under its belt, it rarely misses a beat. Big international names such as Chano Domínguez, Tal Farlow and Wynton Marsalis have all played here, and there's everything from Latin jazz and fusion to tango and classical jazz. Shows start at 10pm and tickets go on sale an hour before the set starts. (☏91 369 41 43; www.cafecentralmadrid.com; Plaza del Ángel 10; admission €10-15; ☺1.30pm-2.30am Sun-Thu, 1.30pm-3.30am Fri & Sat; Ⓜ Antón Martín, Sol)

Teatro de la Zarzuela   THEATRE

23 ⭐ Map p54, D3

This theatre, built in 1856, is the premier place to see *zarzuela*, a singing, dancing, operatic theatre form particular to Madrid. It also hosts smattering of classical music and c era, as well as the Compañía Nacic de Danza. (☏91 524 54 00; http://teatr delazarzuela.mcu.es; Calle de Jovellanos 4 tickets €5-42; ☺box office noon-6pm Mo 3-6pm Sat & Sun; Ⓜ Banco de España)

Sala El Sol   LIVE M

24 ⭐ Map p54, B2

Madrid institutions don't come any more beloved than Sala El Sol. It opened in 1979, just in time for *la movida madrileña,* and quickly es lished itself as a leading stage for a the icons of the era. *La movida* ma have faded into history, but it lives at El Sol, where the music rocks an rolls and usually resurrects the '70 and '80s. After the show, DJs spin rock, fusion and electronica from t awesome sound system. (☏91 532 6 90; www.elsolmad.com; Calle de los Jardín 3; admission €8-25; ☺11pm-5.30am Tue-Jul-Sep; Ⓜ Gran Vía)

Villa Rosa   FLAME

25 ⭐ Map p54, B4

The extraordinary tiled facade of th longstanding nightclub is a tourist attraction in itself. It's been going strong since 1914 and has seen ma manifestations – it made its name a flamenco venue and has recently returned to its roots with well-pric shows and meals that won't break the bank. (☏91 521 36 89; Plaza de San

…erformance of *El Rey que Rabió*, Teatro de la Zarzuela

5; admission €17; ⊘shows 8.30pm &
…pm Sun-Thu, 8.30pm, 10.45pm & 12.15am
…Sat, 11pm-6am Mon-Sat; **M**Sol)

…stello Café &
…eclub   LIVE MUSIC

Map p54, B2

…cool. Costello Café & Niteclub
…nooth-as-silk ambience wedded
…an innovative mix of pop, rock
…fusion in Warholesque surrounds.
…'s live music at 9.30pm every
…t of the week except Sundays, with
…lent and visiting DJs keeping you
…our feet until closing time from
…rsday to Saturday. (www.costelloclub
…Calle del Caballero de Gracia 10; admis-
…€5-10; ⊘6pm-1am Sun-Wed, 6pm-2.30am
…at; **M**Gran Vía)

Cardamomo   FLAMENCO

27 ⭐ Map p54, C3

One of the better flamenco stages
in town, Cardamomo draws more
tourists than aficionados, but the
flamenco is top-notch. (☎91 369 07
57; www.cardamomo.es; Calle de Echegaray
15; admission incl drink €32, incl meal €68;
⊘10pm-3.30am daily, live shows 9pm Tue-
Sun; **M**Sevilla)

Shopping

Casa de Diego   ACCESSORIES

28 🔒 Map p54, A3

This classic shop has been around
since 1858, making, selling and repair-
ing Spanish fans, shawls, umbrellas

Understand

Pedro Almodóvar

Born in a small, impoverished village in Castilla-La Mancha, Almodóvar once remarked that in such conservative rural surrounds, 'I felt as if I'd fallen from another planet'. After he moved to Madrid in 1969 he found his spiritual home and began his career making underground Super-8 movies and making a living by selling secondhand goods at El Rastro flea market. His early films *Pepi, Luci, Bom y Otras Chicas del Montón* (*Pepi, Luci, Bom and the Other Girls*; 1980) and *Laberinto de Pasiones* (*Labyrinth of Passions*; 1982) – the film that brought a young Antonio Banderas to attention – announced him as the icon of *la movida madrileña*, the explosion of hedonism and creativity in the early years of post-Franco Spain. Almodóvar had both in bucketloads; he peppered his films with candy-bright colours and characters leading lives where sex and drugs were the norm. By night Almodóvar performed in Madrid's most famous *movida* bars as part of a drag act called Almodóvar & McNamara. He even appeared in this latter role in *Laberinto de Pasiones*

By the mid-1980s *madrileños* had adopted him as one of the city's most famous sons and he went on to broaden his fanbase with quirkily comic looks at modern Spain, generally set in the capital, such as *Mujeres al Borde de un Ataque de Nervios* (*Women on the Verge of a Nervous Breakdown*; 1988) and *¡Átame!* (*Tie Me Up! Tie Me Down!*; 1990). *Todo Sobre Mi Madre* (*All About My Mother*; 1999) won Almodóvar his first Oscar for Best Foreign Film and is also notable for the coming of age of the Madrid-born actress Penélope Cruz, who had starred in a number of Almodóvar films and was considered part of a select group of the director's leading ladies long before she became a Hollywood star. Other outstanding movies in a formidable portfolio include *Tacones Lejanos* (*High Heels;* 1991) in which Villa Rosa (p60) makes an appearance; *Hable Con Ella* (*Talk to Her*; 2002), for which he won a Best Original Screenplay Oscar; and *Volver* (*Return*; 2006), which reunited Almodóvar with Penélope Cruz to popular and critical acclaim.

canes; the fans are works of art.
.casadediego.com; Plaza de la Puerta del
; ☻9.30am-8pm Mon-Sat; Ⓜ Sol)

é Ramírez

MUSIC

🅐 Map p54, A4

Ramírez is one of Spain's best
r makers and his guitars have
strummed by a host of flamenco
s and international musicians
n the Beatles). This is craftsman-
of the highest order. (📞 91 531
; www.guitarrasramirez.com; Calle de
8; ☻10am-2pm & 4.30-8pm Mon-Fri,
am-2pm Sat; Ⓜ Sol)

ACCESSORIES

🅐 Map p54, B3

don't see them much these days,
he exquisite fringed and embroi-
d *mantones* and *mantoncillos*
litional Spanish shawls worn
omen on grand occasions) and
ate *mantillas* (Spanish veils) are
ning and uniquely Spanish gifts.
lso sells *abanicos* (Spanish fans).
era de San Jerónimo 2; ☻9.30am-
m & 4.30-8pm Mon-Sat; Ⓜ Sol)

Lomography

GIFTS

31 🅐 Map p54, C3

Dedicated to the Lomo LC-A, a 1980s-
era Russian Kompakt camera that
has acquired cult status for its zany
colours, fisheye lenses and anticool
clunkiness, this eclectic shop sells the
cameras (an original will set you back
€295) and offbeat design items, from
bags and mugs to retro memorabilia
loved by adherents of 'lomography'.
(📞 91 369 17 99; www.lomography.com;
Cuesta de Echegaray 5; ☻11am-8.30pm Mon-
Fri; Ⓜ Sevilla, Sol)

María Cabello

WINE

32 🅐 Map p54, C4

This family-run corner shop really
knows its wines and the decoration
has scarcely changed since 1913, with
wooden shelves and even a faded
ceiling fresco. There are fine wines
in abundance, with some 500 labels
on show or tucked away out the back.
(Calle de Echegaray 19; ☻9.30am-2.30pm
& 5.30-9pm Mon-Fri, 10am-2.30pm & 6.30-
9.30pm Sat; Ⓜ Sevilla, Antón Martín)

Explore

El Retiro & the Art Museums

Madrid's golden mile of art takes in three of Europe's most prestigious and rewarding art galleries, nicely carving up between them centuries of European art. Galleries aside, the Paseo del Prado is a gracious tree-lined boulevard of singular beauty, lined with museums and gardens. Away to the east, the Parque del Buen Retiro is one our favourite places in the city.

e Sights in a Day

Get to the **Museo del Prado** (p66) for opening time to avoid crowds; spend at least two hours e museum, more if you don't plan turn on another day. When you ly tear yourself away, rest in the Jardín Botánico, before lunching ome of Madrid's most innovative s at **Estado Puro** (p83).

It would be overkill to attempt all three of the major galleries single day, so choose between the eo Thyssen-Bornemisza (p76) oad journey through the world of pean art) and the **Centro de Arte a Sofía** (p72) (contemporary art, ding Picasso's *Guernica*). After uple of hours at the gallery of choice, visit the **Iglesia de San nimo El Real** (p71) and **Plaza a Cibeles** (p83) en route to the ue del Buen Retiro (p80) – spend ng wandering through these glori-gardens as you can.

After dinner at **Viridiana** (p83), **Kapital** (p83) is your only n for nightlife, although it often n't open until midnight. Fortunate- s worth waiting for and the bars of tas are right next door to help you the time.

Getting There

Ⓜ **Metro** The two main stations for the Paseo del Prado and the art museums are: at the northern end, Banco de España station (line 2) sits on Plaza de la Cibeles – getting out here means a slightly downhill walk to the museums; at the southern end, Atocha station (line 1) is very close to the Centro de Arte Reina Sofía.

Top Sights
Museo del Prado

Welcome to one of the world's premier art galleries. The more than 7000 paintings held in the Museo del Prado's collection (although only around 1500 are on display at any one time) are like a window into the historical vagaries of the Spanish soul, at once grand and imperious in the royal paintings of Velázquez, darkly tumultuous in Goya's *Pinturas Negras* (Black Paintings) and outward-looking with sophisticated works of art from all across Europe.

◉ Map p82, B3

www.museodelprado

Paseo del Prado

adult/child €12/free, 6-8pm Mon-Sat & 5-7 Sun, audioguides €3.

🕙10am-8pm Mon-Sa 10am-7pm Sun

Ⓜ Banco de España

Goya's *La Maja Desnuda* (p69), Museo del Prado

on't Miss

Dos de Mayo (Goya)

a is on all three floors of the Prado, but begin
he southern end of the ground or lower level.
ooms 64 and 65, Goya's *El Dos de Mayo* and
res de Mayo rank among Madrid's most
blematic paintings; they bring to life the 1808
-French revolt and subsequent execution of
rgents in Madrid.

turas Negras (Goya)

ooms 66 and 67, Goya's disturbing 'Black
atings' are so named for the distorted ani-
esque appearance of their characters. The
urno Devorando a Su Hijo (Saturn Devour-
His Son) evokes a writhing mass of tortured
nanity, while *La Romería de San Isidro* and
elarre (El Gran Cabrón) are dominated by the
pelling individual faces of the condemned
ls.

Coloso

nteresting footnote to *Pinturas Negras*
l Coloso, a Goyaesque work that was long
sidered part of the master's portfolio until the
lo's experts decided otherwise in 2008. The
ating and its story are found adjacent to the
k Paintings.

Família de Carlos IV (Goya)

s painting is a small fragment of Spanish
ory transferred to canvas. It shows the royal
ily in 1800 with Fernando (later Fernando
dressed in blue on the left. His fiancée has
been yet chosen, which may be why Goya
icts her with no facial definition. Goya
trayed himself in the background just as
zquez did in *Las Meninas*.

☑ Top Tips

▶ Avoid the free open-
ing hours (crowds
can really spoil your
visit) – first thing in the
morning is best.

▶ Whether you enter
from the west or north,
tickets must be pur-
chased from the ticket
office at the building's
northern end.

▶ The free plan lists the
location of 50 Prado
masterpieces and gives
room numbers for all
major artists.

▶ Plan to make a couple
of visits as the Prado can
be a little overwhelming
if you try to absorb it all
at once.

✗ Take a Break

Across the other side
of the Paseo del Prado,
Estado Puro (p83) is
one of Madrid's most
exciting tapas bars,
with innovative twists
on traditional Spanish
mainstays.

The cafe inside the
Museo del Prado
serves reasonable
cafeteria-style meals
and snacks.

Museo del Prado

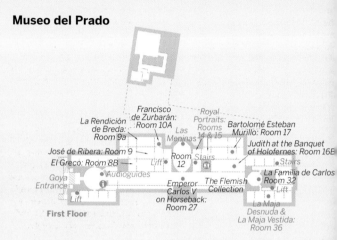

Francisco de Zurbarán: Room 10A
Royal Portraits: Rooms 14 & 15
Bartolomé Esteban Murillo: Room 17
La Rendición de Breda: Room 9a
Las Meninas
Judith at the Banquet of Holofernes: Room 16B
José de Ribera: Room 9
Room 12
Stairs
Stairs
El Greco: Room 8B
Lift
La Familia de Carlos IV: Room 32
Goya Entrance
Audioguides
Emperor Carlos V on Horseback: Room 27
The Flemish Collection
Lift
Lift
La Maja Desnuda & La Maja Vestida: Room 36

First Floor

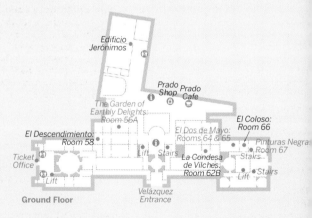

Edificio Jerónimos

Prado Shop
Prado Cafe

The Garden of Earthly Delights: Room 56A

El Coloso: Room 66

El Descendimiento: Room 58

El Dos de Mayo: Rooms 64 & 65

Pinturas Negras: Room 67

Ticket Office

Lift
Stairs

La Condesa de Vilches: Room 62B

Stairs

Lift

Lift

Velázquez Entrance

Ground Floor

re Goya...

he 1st floor, there are more Goyas.
ong them are two more of Goya's
-known and most intriguing oils:
Maja Vestida and *La Maja Desnuda*.
se portraits of an unknown woman,
monly believed to be the Duquesa
lba (who some think may have
 Goya's lover), are identical save
he lack of clothing in the latter.

Meninas (Velázquez)

ll the works by Velázquez, *Las
inas* (Room 12) is what most peo-
ome to see. Completed in 1656,
picts the infant Margarita. The
st portrays himself painting the
; and queen, whose images appear,
rding to some experts, in mirrors
nd Velázquez. His mastery of light
colour is never more apparent
 here.

al Portraits (Velázquez)

rooms surrounding *Las Meninas
ms 14 and 15) contain more
works by Velázquez. Watch in
icular for his paintings of various
bers of royalty who seem to
ng off the canvas – Felipe II, Felipe
Margarita de Austria (a younger
ion of whom features in *Las Meni-
*, El Príncipe Baltasar Carlos and
el de Francia – on horseback.

Rendición de Breda
lázquez)

ázquez's masterpiece shows the
ent in 1625 in which Spanish
eral Ambrosio Spinola accepts the
surrender of the Dutch town of Breda
after a long siege. The Spanish novel-
ist Arturo Pérez-Reverte mixed fantasy
and reality in his novel *The Sun Over
Breda*, claiming that his character
Captain Alatriste appeared in the
painting but was later mysteriously
erased by Velázquez.

Other Spanish Masters

If Spanish painters have piqued your
curiosity, Bartolomé Esteban Murillo,
José de Ribera and the stark figures of
Francisco de Zurbarán should be on
your itinerary. The vivid, almost surreal
works by the 16th-century master and
adopted Spaniard El Greco, whose figures are characteristically slender and
tortured, are also perfectly executed.

La Condesa de Vilches (Madrazo)

The painter was a friend of the model
which may be why he is able to trans-
mit all her grace and sensuality. The
light blue dress, the tone of her skin,
the brightness in her eyes and the
smile slightly pointed suggest a time-
less sympathy that endures through
the centuries.

The Flemish Collection

The Prado's outstanding collection
of Flemish art includes the fulsome
figures and bulbous cherubs of Peter
Paul Rubens (1577–1640). His signature works are *Las Tres Gracias* and
Adoración de los Reyes Magos. Other
fine works in the vicinity include *The
Triumph of Death* by Pieter Bruegel
and those by Anton Van Dyck.

Understand
The Life & Times of Goya

Francisco José de Goya y Lucientes (1746–1828) started his career as a cartoonist in Madrid's Royal Tapestry Workshop. In 1792, illness left him deaf; many critics speculate that his condition was largely responsible for his wild, often merciless style that would become increasingly unshackled from convention. By 1799 Goya was appointed Carlos IV's court painter.

After painting his enigmatic masterpieces *La Maja Vestida* and *La Maja Desnuda*, and the frescoes in Madrid's Ermita de San Antonio de la Florida, the arrival of the French and war in 1808 had a profound impact on Goya; *El Dos de Mayo* and, more dramatically, *El Tres de Mayo* are unforgiving portrayals of the brutality of war.

After he retired to the Quinta del Sordo (Deaf Man's House) west of the Río Manzanares in Madrid, he created his nightmarish *Pinturas Negras* (Black Paintings). Executed on the walls of the house, they were later removed and now hang in the Prado. Goya spent the last years of his life in voluntary exile in France, where he continued to paint until his death.

El Descendimiento (Van Der Weyden)

This 1435 painting is unusual, both for its size and for the recurring crossbow shapes in the painting's upper corners which are echoed in the bodies of Mary and Christ (the painting was commissioned by a Crossbow Man[u]facturers Brotherhood). Once the central part of a triptych, the paint[ing] is filled with drama and luminous colours.

The Garden of Earthly Delights (Bosch)

On no account miss the weird and wonderful *The Garden of Earthly Delights* (Room 56A) by Hieronym[us] Bosch (c 1450–1516). No one has ye[t] been able to provide a definitive ex[]planation for this hallucinatory wo[rk] although many have tried. The clos[er] you look, the harder it is to escape [the] feeling that he must have been doi[ng] some extraordinary drugs.

El Greco

This Greek-born artist (hence the name) is considered the finest of th[e] Prado's Spanish Renaissance painte[rs] Two of his more than thirty paintin[gs] in the collection – *The Annunciatio[n]* and *The Flight into Egypt* – were painted in Italy before the artist ar[]rived in Spain, while *The Trinity* a[nd] *Knight with His Hand on his Breas[t]* are considered his most important works.

Judith at the Banquet of Holofernes (Rembrandt)

The only painting by Rembrandt in the Prado's collection was complete[d] in 1634; note the artist's signature and date on the arm of the chair. Th[]

nting shows a master at the peak of
powers, with a masterly use of the
aroscuro style, and the astonishing
ail in the subject's clothing and
e.

**peror Carlos V on
rseback (Titian)**

nsidered one of the finest eques-
an and royal portraits in art his-
y, this 16th-century work is said to
the forerunner to similar paintings
Velázquez a century later. One of
great masters of the Renaissance,
ian (1488–1576) was entering his
st celebrated period as a painter
en he created this, and it is widely
ognised as one of his masterpieces.

e Best of the Rest…

matter how long you spend in the
ado, there's always more to discover.
ch as the paintings by Dürer, Rafael,
ntoretto, Sorolla, Gainsborough, Fra
gelico, Tiepolo…

ificio Villanueva

e western wing (Edificio Villanue-
) was completed in 1785 as the
oclassical Palacio de Villanueva.
served as a cavalry barracks for
poleon's troops between 1808 and
13. In 1814 King Fernando VII de-
ed to use the palace as a museum.
e years later the Museo del Prado
ened with 311 Spanish paintings on
splay.

Edificio Jerónimos

The Prado's eastern wing (Edificio
Jerónimos) is part of the Prado's stunning modern extension. Dedicated
to temporary exhibitions (usually to
display Prado masterpieces held in
storage for decades for lack of wall
space), its main attraction is the 2nd-
floor cloisters. Built in 1672 with local
granite, the cloisters were until recently attached to the adjacent Iglesia
de San Jerónimo El Real.

Casón del Buen Retiro

This building overlooking the Parque
del Buen Retiro is run as an academic
library by the nearby Museo del Prado.
The Prado runs guided visits to the
stunning Hall of the Ambassadors,
which is crowned by the astonishing
1697 ceiling fresco *The Apotheosis of the
Spanish Monarchy* by Luca Giordano.

Iglesia de San Jerónimo El Real

Tucked away behind the Museo del
Prado, this **chapel** (📞 91 420 35 78; Calle
de Ruiz de Alarcón; 🕙 10am-1pm & 5-8.30pm
Mon-Sat Oct-Jun, hours vary Jul-Sep; Ⓜ Atocha, Banco de España) was traditionally
favoured by the Spanish royal family,
and King Juan Carlos I was crowned
here in 1975 upon the death of Franco.
The sometimes-sober, sometimes-
splendid mock-Isabelline interior is
actually a 19th-century reconstruction.
What remained of the former cloisters
has been incorporated into the Museo
del Prado.

Top Sights
Centro de Arte Reina Sofía

Home to Picasso's *Guernica*, arguably Spain's single-most famous artwork, and a host of other important Spanish artists, the Centro de Arte Reina Sofía is Madrid's premier collection of contemporary art. In addition to plenty of paintings by Picasso, other major drawcards are works by Salvador Dalí and Joan Miró. The collection principally spans the 20th century up to the 1980s, and although the occasional non-Spaniard artist makes an appearance, most of the collection is strictly peninsular.

◉ Map p82, A5

www.museoreinasofia

Calle de Santa Isabel 5

adult/concession €6/
free, free Sun, 7-9pm
Mon-Fri & 2.30-9pm S

⊗10am-9pm Mon-Sa
10am-2.30pm Sun

Ⓜ Atocha

Picasso's *Guernica*, Centro de Arte Reina Sofía

on't Miss

ernica (Picasso)

aimed by some to be the single-most impor-
t artwork of the 20th century, Pablo Picasso's
rnica is an icon of the cubist style for which
asso became famous. You could easily spend
urs studying the painting, but take the time to
h examine the detail of its various constitu-
elements and step back to get an overview of
extraordinary canvas.

eparatory Sketches

deepen your understanding of *Guernica*,
't neglect the sketches that Picasso painted
he prepared to execute his masterpiece.
y're found in the rooms surrounding
m 206 (allowing you to move between and
npare the sketches and main painting with
e). They offer an intriguing insight into the
clopment of this seminal work.

her Cubist Masters

asso may have been the brainchild behind the
ist form, but he was soon joined by others
o saw its potential. Picasso is said to have
n influenced by the mask traditions of Africa,
these elements can also be discerned in
work of Madrid-born Juan Gris (1887–1927)
Georges Braque (1882–1963), two of the
oubted masters of the genre.

an Miró

work of Joan Miró (1893–1983) is defined by
en delightfully bright primary colours. Since
paintings became a symbol of the Barcelona
mpics in 1992, his work has begun to receive
international acclaim it so richly deserves
the museum is a fine place to get a repre-
tative sample of his innovative work.

☑ Top Tips

▶ The permanent
collection is on the 2nd
and 4th floors of the
museum's main wing,
the Edificio Sabatini.

▶ *Guernica*'s location
(Room 206, 2nd floor)
never changes.

▶ The Reina Sofía's
paintings are grouped
together by theme
rather than artist – pick
up a copy of the *Planos
de Museo* (Museum
Floorplans).

▶ The museum's *Guide
to the Collection* (€22),
available from the gift
shop, takes a closer look
at 80 of the museum's
signature works.

✗ Take a Break

Visible from the mu-
seum's entrance, **El
Brillante** (Calle del Doctor
Drumén 7; bocadillos €4.50-
6.50, raciones €7.50-12;
⏱6.30am-12.30am; Ⓜ Ato-
cha) is a breezy, no-frills
bar-eatery. It's a
Madrid institution for
its *bocadillos* (filled
rolls, especially the
ones stuffed with ca-
lamari) and *chocolate
con churros* (deep-
fried doughnut strips).

Salvador Dalí

The Reina Sofía is also home to around 20 canvases by Salvador Dalí (1904–89), of which the most famous is perhaps the surrealist extravaganza *El Gran Masturbador* (1929); at once disturbing and utterly compelling, this is one of the museum's stand-out paintings. Look also for a strange bust of a certain Joelle done by Dalí and his friend Man Ray.

More Surrealism

Dalí aside, the Reina Sofía doesn't have many surrealist paintings, but just as lesser-known masters of the cubist style provide a reference point for Picasso, so too does Max Ernst (1891–1976) provide an intriguing counterpoint to Dalí. His sculpture *La Bella Alemana* (1934–35) is typical of his style.

Contemporary Spanish Artists I

If you can tear yourself away from the big names, the Reina Sofía offers a terrific opportunity to learn more about lesser-known 20th-century Spanish artists. Among these are: Miquel Barceló (b 1957); *madrileño* artist José Gutiérrez Solana (1886–1945), the renowned Basque painter Ignazio Zuloaga (1870–1945) and Benjamín Palencia (1894–1980), whose paintings capture the turbulence of Spain in the 1930s.

Contemporary Spanish Artists II

The late Barcelona painter Antoni Tàpies (1923–2012), for years one of Spain's most creative and extraordinary talents, is represented, as is the pop art of Eduardo Arroyo (b 1937), abstract painters such as Eusebio Sempere (1923–85) and members of the Equipo 57 group (founded in 19 by a group of Spanish artists in exil in Paris), including Pablo Palazuelo (1916–2007).

Lorca

As always, Federico García Lorca (1898–1936) belongs in a class of hi own. Although better known as a p and playwright, he is represented i the Reina Sofía by a number of his sketches.

Sculptures

Of the sculptors, watch in particula for Pablo Gargallo (1881–1934), who work in bronze includes a bust of Picasso, and the renowned Basque sculptors Jorge Oteiza (1908–2003) and Eduardo Chillida (1924–2002). Chillida's sculptures, rendered in rusted wrought-iron, are among Spanish art's most intriguing (and pleasing) forms.

Architecture

Beyond its artwork, the Reina Sofía an important architectural landma adapted from the shell of an 18th-century hospital with eye-catching external glass lifts. The stunning extension (the Edificio Nouvel) tha spreads along the western tip of th Plaza del Emperador Carlos V, host temporary exhibitions, auditoriums the bookshop, a cafe and the museum's library.

Understand
Picasso's Guernica
--- --- --- --- --- --- --- --- --- --- --- ---

Guernica is one of the most famous paintings in the world, a signature work of cubism whose disfiguration of the human form would become an eloquent symbol of a world's outrage at the horrors wrought upon the innocent by modern warfare. For some it's an overtly political work, a moment captured in time when the world lost its innocence. For others it is the painting that announced the arrival (and remains the most enduring symbol) of an entirely new genre.

After the Spanish Civil War broke out in 1936, Picasso was commissioned by the Republican government of Madrid to do the painting for the Paris Exposition Universelle in 1937. As news filtered out about the bombing of Gernika (Guernica) in the Basque Country by Hitler's Legión Condor at the request of Franco, Picasso committed his anger to canvas. At least 200 people (possibly many more) died in the 26 April 1937 attack and much of the town was destroyed. To understand the painting's earth-shattering impact at the time, it must be remembered that the attack on Guernica represented the first use of airborne military hardware to devastating effect, and served as a precursor to the devastation wrought by weapons of mass destruction in WWII.

Guernica has always been a controversial work and was initially derided by many as being more propaganda than art – Picasso was no friend of Franco's and he would spend much of his later life in exile. The 3.5m by 7.8m painting subsequently migrated to the USA where it spent time in numerous museums across the country. It only returned to Spain in 1981, in keeping with Picasso's wish that the painting return to Spanish shores only once democracy had been restored.

Given the subject matter, the Basques believe that its true home is in the Basque Country and calls to have it moved there continue unabated. Such a move is, however, unlikely to happen any time soon with the Reina Sofía arguing that the painting is too fragile to be moved again.

Top Sights
Museo Thyssen-Bornemisza

One of the most extraordinary private collections of predominantly European art in the world, the Museo Thyssen-Bornemisza is a worthy member of Madrid's 'Golden Triangle' of art. Where the Museo del Prado or Centro de Arte Reina Sofía enable you to study the body of work of a particular artist in depth, the Thyssen is a place to immerse yourself in a breathtaking breadth of artistic styles. Not surprisingly, it often ends up being many visitors' favourite Madrid art gallery.

◉ Map p82, A2

www.museothyssen.o

Paseo del Prado 8

adult/child €9/free

🕙 10am-7pm Tue-Sun

Ⓜ Banco de España

Exhibition hall, Museo Thyssen-Bornemisza

on't Miss

ligious Art

e 2nd floor, which is home to medieval art, in-
des some real gems hidden among the mostly
h- and 14th-century and predominantly Italian,
rman and Flemish religious paintings and trip-
hs. Much of it is sacred art that won't appeal to
ryone, but it somehow captures the essence of
dieval Europe.

oms 5 & 10

less you've a specialist's eye for the paintings
t fill the first four rooms, pause for the first
e in Room 5 where you'll find one work by
y's Piero della Francesca (1410–92) and the
antly recognisable *Portrait of King Henry VIII*
Holbein the Younger (1497–1543), before con-
uing on to Room 10 for the evocative 1586 *Mas-
re of the Innocents* by Lucas Van Valckenborch.

ain & Venice

om 11 is dedicated to El Greco (with three
ces) and his Venetian contemporaries Tintoretto
l Titian, while Caravaggio and the Spaniard José
Ribera dominate Room 12. A single painting
h by Murillo and Zurbarán add further Spanish
our in the two rooms that follow, while the ex-
tionally rendered views of Venice by Canaletto
97–1768) should on no account be missed.

ropean Masters

t of all on the top floor is the extension
oms A to H) which houses the collection of
men Thyssen-Bornemisza; the rest belonged
er late husband, Baron Thyssen-Bornemisza,
erman-Hungarian magnate. Room C houses
ntings by Canaletto, Constable and Van Gogh,
le the stunning Room H includes works by
net, Sisley, Renoir, Pissarro and Degas.

☑ Top Tips

▶ Don't come here ex-
pecting a large number
of paintings from a sin-
gle master, but instead
expect single paintings
from a large number of
masters.

▶ The collection's oldest
works are on the top
floor, with contemporary
art on the ground floor.
For a journey through
the history of art, start
on the 2nd floor and
work your way down.

▶ The excellent audio-
guide allows you to zero
in on particular paint-
ings, which counters
the feeling of being
overwhelmed by such a
wide-ranging collection.

✗ Take a Break

Estado Puro (p83), just
around the roundabout
within sight of the
museum entrance, is
sophisticated and a
relentlessly creative
tapas bar.

For something a little
more earthy and ec-
lectic, Los Gatos (p57)
also does tapas but
with a more traditional
slant.

Museo Thyssen-Bornemizsa

Second Floor

Flemish Masters:
Rooms 19 to 21

European Masters:
Rooms A to H

Caravaggio &
José de Ribera:
Room 12

Massacre
of the
Innocents

El Greco,
Tintoretto &
Titian: Room 11

Portrait of
King Henry VIII

First Floor

Baroness Collection:
Rooms I to P

Goya:
Room 31

Picasso, Matisse,
Cézanne, Gauguin,
Munch: Rooms
33 to 35

Van Gogh, Manet,
Monet, Pisarro
& Renoir:
Room 32

Gainsborough:
Room 28

Ground Floor

Audioguides

Cubism &
Surrealism:
Rooms
41 to 44

Contemporary
Icons: Rooms
46 to 48

Ticket Office

Shop

Chagall & Dalí:
Room 45

tch & Flemish Masters

ore heading downstairs to the 1st
r, a detour to Rooms 19 through to 21
 satisfy those devoted to 17th-century
ch and Flemish masters, Anton Van
k, Jan Brueghel the Elder, Rubens
 Rembrandt (one painting).

nsborough & Goya

ll that sounds impressive, the
floor is where the Thyssen really
es. There's a Gainsborough in
m 28 and a Goya in Room 31, but
n these are considered secondary
what's around the corner.

om 32

ou've been skimming the surface,
m 32 is the place to linger over
ry painting. The astonishing
ure of Van Gogh's *Les Vessenots* is
asterpiece, but the same applies
Woman in Riding Habit by Manet,
net's *The Thaw at Véthueil*, Renoir's
man with a Parasol in a Garden,
 Pissarro's *Rue Saint-Honoré in the
rnoon*. Simply extraordinary.

oms 33 to 35

re's no time to catch your breath,
ause Room 33 is similarly some-
g special with Cézanne, Gauguin,
louse-Lautrec and Degas all on
w. The big names continue in
m 34 (Picasso, Matisse and Mod-
ani) and 35 (Edvard Munch and
n Schiele).

e Baroness Collection

he 1st floor's extension (Rooms I to
Room K has works by Monet, Pis-
o, Sorolla and Sisley, while Room

L is the domain of Gauguin (including his iconic *Mata Mua*), Degas and
Toulouse-Lautrec. Rooms M (Munch),
N (Kandinsky), O (Matisse and Georges Braque) and P (Picasso, Matisse,
Edward Hopper and Juan Gris) round
out an outrageously rich journey.

Cubism & Surrealism

Down on the ground floor, in Room 41
you'll see a nice mix of the big three of
cubism, Picasso, Georges Braque and
Madrid's own Juan Gris, along with
several other contemporaries. Kandinsky is the main drawcard in Room 43,
while there's an early Salvador Dalí
alongside Max Ernst and Paul Klee in
Room 44.

Room 45

Picasso appears again in Room 45,
another one of the gallery's stand-out
rooms; its treasures include works
by Marc Chagall and Dalí's hallucinatory *Dream Caused by the Flight of a
Bee Around a Pomegranate a Second
Before Waking Up*.

Contemporary Icons

There's no let-up as the Thyssen
builds to a stirring climax. Room 46
has Joan Miró's *Catalan Peasant with
a Guitar*, Jackson Pollock's *Brown
and Silver I* and the deceptively simple but strangely pleasing *Green on
Maroon* by Mark Rothko. In Rooms 47
and 48, Francis Bacon, Roy Lichten-
stein, Henry Moore and Lucian Freud,
Sigmund's Berlin-born grandson, are
all represented.

Top Sights
Parque del Buen Retiro

The glorious gardens of El Retiro are as beautiful as any you'll find in a European city. Laid out in the 17th century by Felipe IV as the preserve of kings, queens and their intimates, the park was opened to the public in 1868 – ever since, it's been a favourite haunt of *madrileños*. Littered with marble monuments, landscaped lawns, the occasional elegant building and abundant greenery, it's quiet and contemplative during the week, but comes to life on weekends.

◉ Map p82, C3

🕑6am-midnight May-Sep, to 11pm Oct-Apr

Ⓜ Retiro, Príncipe de Vergara, Ibiza, Atocha

Lake and Palacio de Cristal, Parque del Buen Retiro

on't Miss

ke (Estanque)

El Retiro focal point, the artificial lake *anque*) is watched over by the massive, amental monument to Alfonso XII, complete h marble lions. Renting a **row boat** (per boat 45min €4.65; ⊙10am-8.30pm Apr-Sep, 10am-5.45pm -Mar) is a very Madrid thing to do.

lacio de Cristal

lden among the trees south of the lake, the acio de Cristal is a magnificent metal and ss pavilion, arguably El Retiro's most beautiful hitectural monument. Built in 1887 as a winter den for exotic flowers, it's now used for tempo-y exhibitions. Its surrounds are our favourite nic spot.

ses & the Devil

the southern end of the park, near La Rosaleda se Garden) with its more than 4000 roses, is a tue of El Ángel Caído (the Fallen Angel), one of v statues to the devil anywhere in the world. It s 666m above sea level...

drid's Oldest Tree

st inside the Puerta de Felipe IV on El Retiro's stern side, stands Madrid's oldest tree, a Mexi-a conifer (*ahuehuete*). Planted in 1633, it was d as a cannon mount by French soldiers dur-; the Napoleonic Wars in the early 19th century.

manesque Ruins

the northeastern corner of the park is the nita de San Isidro, one of the few, albeit modest mples of Romanesque architecture in Madrid. rts of the wall, a side entrance and part of the se were restored in 1999 and are all that remain he 13th-century building. When it was built drid was a small village more than 2km away.

☑ Top Tips

▶ If you're going to rent a boat on weekends, do so around 3pm to 4pm when most locals are having lunch.

▶ Pack a picnic lunch and find an unoccupied stretch of lawn.

▶ Cycling or roller-blading is a terrific way to range far and wide across El Retiro. **By Bike** (www.bybike.info; Avenida de Menédez Pelayo 35; per hr/ day from €4/30; ⊙10am-9pm Mon-Fri & 9.30am-9.30pm Sat & Sun Jun-Sep, reduced hours Oct-May; Ⓜ Ibiza) rents both forms of transport and is just across the road from El Retiro's eastern edge.

✕ Take a Break

Ideal for a picnic lunch, but also a pleasant cafe in its own right, Mallorca (p95) is a fine pit-stop en route to or from the park.

Kiosks sell pricey drinks and there are cafes around the park, but little food for sale – another reason we recommend bringing your own.

A

Plaza del Rey

CENTRO

Banco de España

Paseo del Prado Ⓜ

C de Alcalá

Ⓜ Banco de España

C de Marqués de Cubas

C de los Madrazo

C de Zorrilla

Museo Thyssen-Bornemisza

Carrera de San Jerónimo

C de Cervantes ✗ 3

Plaza de Jesús

C del Duque de Medinaceli

C de Lope de Vega

HUERTAS

C de las Huertas

C de Moratín

C del Gobernador

C de Fúcar

C de la Alameda

C de Ceñicero

C de Atocha

C de Santa Isabel

Centro de Arte Reina Sofía ◉

C Hospital

LAVAPIÉS

C del Doctor Drumen

Ⓜ Atocha

B

Paseo de los Recoletos

C de Salustiano

C de Sagasta

2 ◉ Plaza de la Cibeles

Paseo del Prado

C de Montalbán

C de Juan de Mena

Plaza de la Lealtad

C de Antonio Maura

Plaza de Neptuno (Plaza de Cánovas del Castillo)

Museo del Prado ◉

C del Duque de Medinaceli

Plaza de Bravo Murillo

JERÓNIMOS

Plaza de Atocha

Real Jardín Botánico

1 ◉ Caixa Forum

C Felipe IV

C de la Academia

C de Morato

C Casado del Alisal

C Alberto Bosch

C de Espalter

C de Ruiz de Alarcón

Cuesta de Claudio Moyano

Ⓜ Atocha

Plaza del Emperador Carlos V

Ⓜ Atocha

Av de la Ciudad de Barcelona

C

JUSTICIA

C de Columela

Retiro Ⓜ

Plaza de la Independencia

Puerta Independencia

Paseo de México

C Valenzuela

C de Alfonso XII

Paseo de Colombia

✗ 4

Paseo de la Argentina

Puerta de España

RETIRO

Parque del Retiro

Paseo Parterre

Puerta Felipe IV

Parque del Buen Retiro ◉

Paseo San Pablo

Jerónimos

Puerta Murillo

C de Alfonso XII

Paseo de Fernán Nuñ

D

C de Alc

C de Alcalá

Puerta Independencia

Estanc

Paseo de la

Jardín de los Plánteles

Paseo de la Infanta Isabel

Atocha Renfe Ⓜ

For reviews see

◉ Top Sights
◉ Sights
✗ Eating
★ Entertainment

N

0   0.1
0

which have their origins in Catalonia's world-famous elBulli restaurant, such as the *tortilla española siglo XXI* (21st-century Spanish omelette, served in a glass). (☑ 91 330 24 00; www.tapasenestado puro.com; Plaza de Cánovas del Castillo 4; tapas €5-12.50; ⊙ 11am-1am Tue-Sat, 11am-4pm Sun; Ⓜ Banco de España, Atocha)

Viridiana   CONTEMPORARY SPANISH €€€

 4 Map p82, C2

The chef here, Abraham García, is a much-celebrated Madrid figure and his larger-than-life personality is reflected in Viridiana's wide-ranging menu. This place was doing fusion cooking long before it became fashionable and has developed a fiercely loyal clientele as a result. In short, it's one of Madrid's best restaurants. (☑ 91 523 44 78; www .restauranteviridiana.com; Calle de Juan de Mena 14; mains €27-37; ⊙ lunch & dinner Mon-Sat; Ⓜ Banco de España)

Entertainment

Kapital   CLUB

5 Map p82, B4

One of the most famous megaclubs in Madrid, this huge seven-storey place has something for everyone: from dance music and cocktail bars to karaoke, salsa, hip hop, chilled spaces for R&B and soul, and 'Made in Spain' music. A cross-section of Madrid society can hang out here without getting in each other's way. (☑ 91 420 29 06; www.grupo -kapital.com; Calle de Atocha 125; admission from €10; ⊙ 5.30-10.30pm & midnight-6am Fri & Sat, midnight-6am Thu & Sun; Ⓜ Atocha)

ights

ixa Forum   MUSEUM, ARCHITECTURE

 Map p82, B4

s extraordinary structure down ards the southern end of the Paseo Prado is one of Madrid's most eye-ching architectural innovations. This ck edifice is topped by an intriguing mit of rusted iron. On an adjacent l is the *jardín colgante* (hanging den), a lush vertical wall of greenery. ide there are four floors of exhibi- n and performance space awash in nless steel and with soaring ceilings. w.fundacio.lacaixa.es; Paseo del Prado 36; ission free; ⊙ 10am-8pm; Ⓜ Atocha)

aza de la Cibeles   SQUARE

Map p82, B1

all the grand roundabouts on the eo del Prado, Plaza de la Cibeles st evokes the splendour of imperial drid. The jewel in the crown is the **lacio de Comunicaciones**. Built Antonio Palacios, Madrid's most lific architect of the belle époque, it ves as Madrid's town hall (*ay- amiento*). The **fountain of the god- ss Cybele** (1780) at the centre of the za is one of Madrid's most beautiful. za de la Cibeles; Ⓜ Banco de España)

ating

tado Puro   TAPAS €

Map p82, A3

lick but casual tapas bar attached to NH Paseo del Prado Hotel, Estado ro serves up fantastic tapas, many of

Explore

Salamanca

The *barrio* of Salamanca is Madrid's most exclusive quarter, a place where stately mansions set back from the street sit alongside boutiques from the big local and international fashion designers, and where the unmistakeable whiff of old money mingles comfortably with the aspirations of Spain's *nouveau riche*. Put on your finest clothes and be seen.

he Sights in a Day

Start your morning at the **Museo Lázaro Galdiano** (p86), n follow Calle de Serrano into the rt of Salamanca, pausing en route he **Museo al Aire Libre** (p92). By time you reach Calle de José Ortega asset, one of Europe's great shop-g streets, you've arrived at Spain's nion central. Meander down for ch at **Restaurante Estay** (p89), **La onial de Goya** (p93) or **La Cocina María Luisa** (p94).

After lunch, shop at **Gallery** (p97), then admire the grand **lioteca Nacional** (p92) and check ;ee if the **Museo Arqueológico cional** (p92) has reopened. Walk the k along Calle de Serrano, shop-g at **Camper** (p88), **Loewe** (p97), **atha Ruiz de la Prada** (p89) and **nolo Blahnik** (p89) among other ns of Spanish fashion.

Salamanca nights are pretty quiet by Madrid standards, but re's still plenty to keep you busy. For re-dinner drink, join the after-work wd at **El Lateral** (p89). If you feel tapas, it's **Biotza** (p94). If you pre-a sit-down meal in classy surrounds, **Sula Madrid** (p93). To dance the ht away, try **Serrano 41** (p95) for an market crowd, or **Almonte** (p95) for nenco tunes.

a local's day in Salamanca, see 3.

◉ Top Sights
Museo Lázaro Galdiano (p86)

◯ Local Life
Shopping in Upmarket Salamanca (p88)

♥ Best of Salamanca

Spanish Fashion
Agatha Ruiz de la Prada (p89)

Camper (p88)

Loewe (p97)

Manolo Blahnik (p89)

Purificación García (p97)

Gourmet Food Shops
Bombonerías Santa (p89)

Oriol Balaguer (p89)

Mantequería Bravo (p97)

Tapas
Biotza (p94)

La Colonial de Goya (p93)

Restaurante Estay (p89)

Getting There

Ⓜ **Metro** For the heart of Salamanca, Serrano (line 4) and Nuñez de Balboa (5 and 9) stations are best. Useful perimeter stations are Goya (2 and 4), Velázquez (4), Príncipe de Vergara (2 and 9), Retiro (2) and Colón (4).

Top Sights
Museo Lázaro Galdiano

This imposing, early-20th-century Italianate stone mansion set discreetly back from the street was once the home of one Don José Lázaro Galdiano (1862–1947), a successful and cultivated businessman. A patron of the arts and quintessential Salamanca personality, he built up an astonishing private collection that he bequeathed to the city upon his death. It was no mean inheritance, with some 13,000 works of art and objets d'art, a quarter of which are on show at any time.

⊙ Map p90, B2

www.flg.es

Calle de Serrano 122

adult/concession €6/ last hr free

⊙10am-4.30pm Wed-Sat & Mon, 10am-3pm Sun

Ⓜ Gregorio Marañón

Museo Lázaro Galdiano

...n't Miss

...ecklist of Old Masters

...n be difficult to believe the breadth of ...terpieces that Señor Lázaro Galdiano gath-... during his lifetime, and there's enough here ...nerit this museum's inclusion among Madrid's ...art galleries. The highlights include works ...Zurbarán, Claudio Coello, Hieronymus Bosch, ...ban Murillo, El Greco, Lucas Cranach and ...stable, and there's even a painting in room 11 ...ibuted to Velázquez.

...ya

...s often the case, Goya belongs in a class of ...own. He dominates room 13, while the ceiling ...he adjoining room 14 features a collage from ...e of Goya's more famous works. Some that ...easy to recognise include *La Maja Desnuda*, ...*Maja Vestida* and the frescoes of the Ermita ...San Antonio de la Florida

...rio Collection

...s remarkable collection, ranging beyond ...ntings to sculptures, bronzes, miniature ...res, jewellery, ceramics, furniture, weapons... ...rly he was a man of wide interests. The ...und floor is largely given over to a display ...ing the social context in which Galdiano lived, ...h hundreds of curios from all around the ...ld on show. There are more on the top floor.

...scoes & Textiles

...lovely 1st floor, which contains many of the ...nish artworks, is arrayed around the centre-...ce of the former ballroom and beneath lavishly ...coed ceilings. And on no account miss the top ...r's room 24, which contains some exquisite ...iles.

☑ Top Tips

▶ Most museums close on Mondays, but this one bucks the trend by closing Tuesday – don't be caught out.

▶ The museum is a long uphill walk from the rest of Salamanca – take the metro here and walk back down.

▶ Unless you've a specialist interest, the guides on sale at the entrance are unnecessary – English and Spanish labelling is excellent.

▶ Seek out the photos of each room to see how it appeared in Galdiano's prime.

✗ Take a Break

José Luis (p94) is where the young and the wealthy come to sip bottled mineral water and order *tortilla de patatas* (Spanish potato omelette). It's across the road from the museum.

Local Life
Shopping in Upmarket Salamanc

From international designers with no need for introductions to Spanish household names that the shopper in you will adore discovering, Salamanca is a fashionista's dream come true. Add some terrific gourmet food purveyors and casual but classy pit stops along the way and it's a day to remember if shopping gets you excited.

1 Camper

Spanish fashion is not all haute couture, and **Camper** (www.camper.e Calle de Serrano 24; ⏰10am-9pm Mon-S 11am-8pm Sun; MSerrano), the world-famous cool and quirky shoe bran from Mallorca, offers bowling-shoe chic with colourful, fun designs th are all about quality coupled with comfort.

Agatha Ruiz de la Prada

Agatha Ruiz de la Prada (www.agatharuiz
prada.com; Calle de Serrano 27; ⏰10am-
⏰m Mon-Sat; Ⓜ Serrano) has to be seen
believed, with pinks, yellows and
ges everywhere. It's fun and exu-
nt, but also has serious and highly
nal fashion.

Bombonerías Santa

n people who live in Salamanca
ooking for a tasteful gift to take to
next dinner party, many of them
e to **Bombonerías Santa** (www
boneras-santa.com; Calle de Serrano 56;
am-8.30pm Mon-Sat Sep-Jun, shorter
in summer; Ⓜ Serrano). And if your
is as refined as your palate, the
isitely presented chocolates here
eason enough to join them, dinner
y or not.

Manolo Blahnik

e's a reason that the world-famous
designer **Manolo Blahnik** (⏰91 575
; www.manoloblahnik.com; Calle de Ser-
8; ⏰10am-8.30pm Mon-Sat; Ⓜ Serrano)
boutique along Calle de Serrano –
nanca's trendy young things make
oint of reference to own a pair.
showroom is exclusive and each
is displayed like a work of art.

Restaurante Estay

tracking slightly to the southeast,
aurante Estay (www.estayrestaurante
Calle de Hermosilla 46; tapas €1.75-5, 6-
set menus from €13.80; ⏰8am-12.30am
Sat; Ⓜ Velázquez) is partly Spanish
where besuited waiters serve *café*
eche, and also one of the best-loved
bars in this part of town. There's
g list of tapas and it's a classy but
place to rest before continuing.

❻ Oriol Balaguer

Catalan pastry chef **Oriol Balaguer**
(www.oriolbalaguer.com; Calle de José Ortega y
Gasset 44; ⏰9am-9pm Mon-Sat, 9am-2.30pm
Sun; Ⓜ Nuñez de Balboa) won a prize for
the World's Best Dessert (the 'Seven
Textures of Chocolate') in 2001. His
chocolate boutique is presented like a
small art gallery dedicated to exquisite,
finely crafted chocolate collections and
cakes.

❼ Calle de José Ortega y Gasset

The world's most prestigious international designers occupy what is known
as *la milla del oro* (the golden mile)
along Calle de José Ortega y Gasset,
close to the corner with Calle de Serrano. On the south side of the street,
there's **Giorgio Armani** (⏰91 577 58 07;
www.armani.com; Calle de José Ortega y Gasset
16; ⏰10am-8pm Mon-Sat) and **Chanel**
(⏰91 431 30 36; www.chanel.com; Calle de
José Ortega y Gasset 14; ⏰10am-8pm Mon-
Sat). Just across the road is **Louis Vuitton** (⏰91 575 13 08; www.louisvuitton.com;
Calle de José Ortega y Gasset 17; ⏰10am-8pm
Mon-Sat) and **Cartier** (⏰91 576 22 81; www
.cartier.com; cnr Calles de José Ortega y Gasset
& de Serrano; ⏰10am-8.30pm Mon-Fri, 11am-
8pm Sat). And that's just the start...

❽ El Lateral

This chic **wine bar** (⏰91 435 06 04;
Calle de Velázquez 57; ⏰noon-1am Sun-Thu,
until late Fri & Sat; Ⓜ Velázquez, Nuñez de
Balboa) is cool in the right places, filled
as it is with slick suits and classic
wines alongside the new wave of style
shaking up the *barrio*. It's a classic
perch along one of Salamanca's main
boulevards to wind down after a hard
day's shopping.

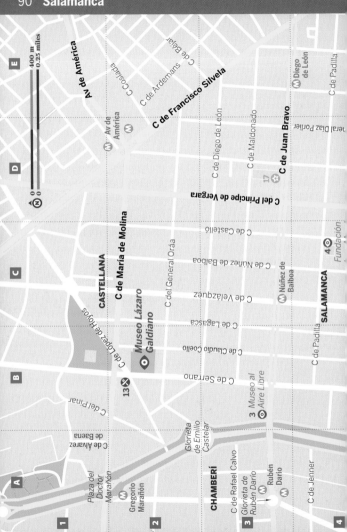

For reviews see	
◉ Top Sights	p86
◐ Sights	p92
✕ Eating	p93
✕ Drinking	p95
⚽ Entertainment	p95
🛍 Shopping	p96

GOYA

RECOLETOS

JUSTICIA

Parque del Retiro

Plaza de Salvador Dalí

Plaza de la Independencia

Hammam ⊙5

C de Alcá

C de Ayala

C de Alca

C del Conde de Peñalver

C de la Hermosilla

C del General Pardiñas

C de Goya

16

C de Alcalá

C del Duque de Sesto

C de O'Donnell

C de Narváez

Goya

Goya

Ibiza

C del General Díaz Porlier

Av de Menéndez Pelayo

C del Príncipe de Vergara

Príncipe de Vergara

Paseo del Duque de Fernán Núñez

C de Jorge Juan

C de Castelló

C de Núñez de Balboa

21 12

C de Villanueva

C de Alcalá

C de Velázquez

Velázquez

20

7

8

C de Ayala

C de la Hermosilla

C de Goya

C de Claudio Coello

C de Jorge Juan

C de Villanueva

C del Conde de Aranda

9

Museo Arqueológico Nacional

10

Chi Spa 6

C de Columela

15

Retiro

C de Salustiano

C de Fernando el Santo

C de Serrano

Serrano

Jardines de Descubrimiento

Biblioteca Nacional & Museo del Libro

24 22

1 2

C de Villanueva

14 del Cid 11

C de los Recoletos

Colón

Paseo de los Recoletos

Paseo de la Cas

Paseo de la Castellana

23

Sights

Biblioteca Nacional & Museo del Libro
LIBRARY, MUSEUM

1 Map p90, A7

Perhaps the most impressive of the grand edifces erected along the Paseo de los Recoletos in the 19th century, the 1892 **Biblioteca Nacional** (National Library) dominates the southern end of Plaza de Colón. Downstairs, the fascinating and recently overhauled **museum**, is a must for bibliophiles. (☏91 580 78 05; www.bne.es; Paseo de los Recoletos 20; admission free; ☉library 9am-9pm Mon-Fri, 9am-2pm Sat, museum 10am-9pm Tue-Sat, 10am-2pm Sun; Ⓜ Colón)

Museo Arqueológico Nacional
MUSEUM

2 Map p90, A7

The showpiece National Archaeology Museum contains a sweeping accumulation of artefacts behind its towering facade. Until late 2012 (and more likely 2013), the museum was closed for a major and much-needed overhaul of the building. (http://man

.mcu.es; Calle de Serrano 13; admission fre ☉9.30am-8pm Tue-Sat, 9.30am-3pm Sur Ⓜ Serrano)

Museo al Aire Libre
SCULP

3 Map p90, B3

This fascinating open-air collection 17 abstract sculptures hides beneat the overpass where Paseo de Eduar Dato crosses Paseo de la Castellana It includes works by the renowned Basque artist Eduardo Chillida, the Catalan master Joan Miró, as well as Eusebio Sempere and Alberto Sánchez, one of Spain's foremost sculptors of the 20th century. (www .munimadrid.es/museoairelibre; cnr Pasec de la Castellana & Paseo de Eduardo Dato; admission free; ☉24hr; Ⓜ Rubén Darío)

Fundación Juan March
MUSEUM, CULTURAL CE

4 Map p90, C4

This foundation organises some of better temporary exhibitions in M. drid each year and it's always wort checking its website to see what's or around the corner. (www.march.es Calle de Castelló 77; admission free; ☉11a 8pm Mon-Sat, 10am-2pm Sun & holidays; Ⓜ Núñez de Balboa)

Hammam Ayala
DA

5 Map p90, E5

Another excellent traditional Arab bath experience, Hammam Ayala offers massages and a range

th treatments within a faithful
eation of a Middle Eastern *ham-*
. All-natural products and the
ory pleasures of exotic oils make
a lovely escape from modern life.
traditional bath ritual costs €50.
.hammamayala.com; Calle de Ayala 126;
am-8pm Tue & Thu, 1-10pm Wed, Fri, Sat,
Ⓜ Manuel Becerra)

Spa
DAY SPA

Ⓞ Map p90, B7

up in a robe and slippers and
are to be pampered in one of
n's best day spas. There are sepa-
areas for men and women, and
ces include a wide range of mas-
s, facials, manicures and pedicures.
, what was it you were stressed
t? (Ⓙ 91 578 13 40; www.thechispa.com;
del Conde de Aranda 6; Ⓢ 10am-9pm
Fri, 10am-6pm Sat; Ⓜ Retiro)

ting

a
rid
CONTEMPORARY SPANISH €€€

Ⓞ Map p90, C7

stronomic temple that combines
ar cooking with clean-lined
istication, Sula Madrid – a super-
sh tapas bar, top-notch restaurant
ham-and-champagne tasting
re all rolled into one – is one of
favourite top-end restaurants
adrid and we're not the only
– when master chef Ferran Adrià

Sula Madrid

was asked to nominate his favourite
restaurant, he chose Sula. (Ⓙ 91 781 61
97; www.sula.es; Calle de Jorge Juan 33; mains
€23.50-27.50, set menus €30-60; Ⓢ lunch &
dinner Mon-Sat; Ⓜ Velázquez)

La Colonial de Goya
TAPAS €

8 Ⓧ Map p90, C7

A mere 63 varieties of canapé should
be sufficient for most, but they also
serve other tapas and main dishes
at this engaging little tapas bar. The
atmosphere is casual, the all-white
decor of wood and exposed brick walls
is classy. (www.restauranterincondegoya.es;
Calle de Jorge Juan 34; tapas €3-4.50; Ⓢ 8am-
midnight Mon-Fri, noon-1am Sat & Sun;
Ⓜ Velázquez)

Biotza

TAPAS, BASQUE €

9 Map p90, B7

This breezy Basque tapas bar is one of the best places in Madrid to sample the creativity of bite-sized *pintxos* as only the Basques can make them. It's the perfect combination of San Sebastián–style tapas and Madrid-style pale-green and red-black decoration and unusual angular benches. (www.biotzarestaurante.com; Calle de Claudio Coello 27; tapas €2.50-3.50; ⏱9am-midnight Mon-Thu, 9am-1am Fri & Sat; Ⓜ Serrano)

La Galette

SPANISH €€

10 Map p90, B7

This lovely little restaurant combines an intimate dining area with checked tablecloths and cuisine that the owner describes as 'baroque vegetarian'. The food (both veg and non-veg) is a revelation, blending creative flavours with a strong base in traditional home cooking. The *croquetas de manzana* (apple croquettes) are a house special-

Top Tip

Pollie-Watch

María Luisa Banzo, the owner of La Cocina, was formerly a prominent figure in the government of conservative Popular Party Prime Minister José María Aznar – keep an eye out for the former PM (also from Castilla y León) and other prominent politicians in her restaurant.

ity. (☎91 576 06 41; Calle del Conde de Aranda 11; mains €9.50-19.50; ⏱lunch & dinner Mon-Sat, lunch Sun; ♪; Ⓜ Retiro)

Le Café

SPANISH

11 Map p90, A7

It can be almost impossible to get a table here at lunchtime on weekday when locals stream in from surrounding offices. The atmosphere is bright and informal and the food is largely traditional Spanish fare (rice dishes are a recurring theme). (www.lecafe. Calle de los Recoletos 13; mains €12-19, set menus €11.50-19; ⏱lunch & dinner Mon- Ⓜ Retiro)

La Cocina de María Luisa

CASTILIAN

12 Map p90, C7

The home kitchen of former parliamentarian María Luisa Banzo has of Salamanca's most loyal following. The cooking is a carefully charted linary journey through Castilla y L accompanied by well-chosen region wines and rustic decor that add m warmth to this welcoming place. (☎ 781 01 80; www.lacocinademarialuisa.es; de Jorge Juan 42; mains €13.90-23.60, tas menu €54; ⏱lunch & dinner Mon-Sat, clo Aug; Ⓜ Velázquez)

José Luis

SPANISH

13 Map p90, B2

With numerous branches around Madrid, José Luis is famous for its fidelity to traditional Spanish reci

ins many people's vote for Ma-
's best *tortilla de patatas* (Spanish
to omelette). (☑91 562 78 61; Calle
errano 89-90; tapas from €5; ☉lunch &
r daily ; Ⓜ Gregorio Marañón)

Mounia MOROCCAN €€

Map p90, A7

of the longest-standing Moroccan
aurants in town, Al-Mounia has
al following. The best couscous
Madrid is a menu highlight, as are
subtly spiced lamb *tagines* (stew
ked in a ceramic pot) and the
lo berebere (Berber roast; €24.50).
1 435 08 28; www.almounia.es; Calle
s Recoletos 5; mains €16-28; ☉lunch
ner Mon-Sat, lunch Sun, closed Aug;
ecoletos)

llorca TAKEAWAY €

Map p90, B7

fine takeaway food, head to Mal-
a, a Madrid institution. Everything
, from gourmet mains to snacks
desserts, is delicious. (☑91 577 18
ww.pasteleria-mallorca.com; Calle de
no 6; ☉9.30am-9pm; Ⓜ Retiro)

inking

e Geographic Club BAR

Map p90, D6

h its elaborate stained-glass
dows, ethno-chic from all over the
ld and laid-back atmosphere, the
graphic Club is an excellent choice

 Top Tip
Taxi Rides
The *barrio* of Salamanca is one of
the more spread out in Madrid,
and while everything can be ac-
complished on foot, it's rare that
the longest taxi ride will cost more
than €5.

in Salamanca for an early evening
drink. (☑91 578 08 62; www.thegeographic
club.com; Calle de Alcalá 141; ☉1pm-2am Sun-
Thu, 1pm-3am Fri & Sat; Ⓜ Goya)

Entertainment

Almonte NIGHTCLUB

17 ⭐ Map p90, D3

If flamenco has captured your soul,
but you're keen to do more than
watch, head to Almonte, where the
young and the beautiful come with
sevillanas (a flamenco dance style)
in their soul and in their feet. Head
downstairs to see the best dancing
and dance if you dare. (☑91 563 25 04;
www.almontesalarociera.com; Calle de Juan
Bravo 35; ☉10pm-5am Sun-Fri, 10pm-6am
Sat; Ⓜ Núñez de Balboa, Diego de León)

Serrano 41 CLUB

18 ⭐ Map p90, B5

If bullfighters, Real Madrid stars and
other A-listers can't drag themselves
away from Salamanca, chances are
that you'll find them here. Danceable

pop and house dominate the most popular Friday and Saturday nights, funk gets a turn on Sunday and it's indie night on Thursday. As you'd imagine, the door policy is stricter than most. (📞91 578 18 65; www.serrano41.com; Calle de Serrano 41; admission €10; ⏰11pm-5.30am Wed-Sun; Ⓜ Serrano)

Shopping

De Viaje   BOOKS

20 🔒 Map p90, B5

Whether you're after a guidebook, a coffee-table tome or travel literature, De Viaje, Madrid's largest travel bookshop, probably has it. It has mostly

Spanish titles, but plenty in Englis well. Staff are helpful and there's a a travel agency. (📞91 577 98 99; www .deviaje.com; Calle de Serrano 41; ⏰10am 8.30pm Mon-Fri, 10.30am-2.30pm & 5-8p Sat; Ⓜ Serrano)

Ekseption
& Eks   CLOTHING, ACCESSORI

20 🔒 Map p90, C6

This elegant showroom store cons ently leads the way with the latest trends, spanning catwalk designs alongside a more informal, though always sophisticated, look. The ur ing theme is urban chic and its lis designer brands includes Balencia

Agatha Ruiz de la Prada (p89)

la Sport, Marc Jacobs and Dries
Noten. (www.ekseption.es; Calle de
...quez 28; ⊙10.30am-2.30pm & 4.30-
...pm Mon-Sat; Ⓜ Velázquez)

...lery
CLOTHING, ACCESSORIES

 Map p90, C7

...stunning showpiece of men's
...ions and accessories (shoes, bags,
...s and the like) is the new Madrid
...nutshell – stylish, brand con-
...us and all about having the right
.. There are creams and fragrances
...dulge the metrosexual in you, as
...as quirkier such as designer
...h helmets. (www.gallerymadrid.com;
...de Jorge Juan 38; ⊙10.30am-8.30pm
...Sat; Ⓜ Príncipe de Vergara, Velázquez)

...we
FASHION

 Map p90, B6

...we is arguably Spain's signature
...in high-end fashion – it's like
...Spanish Louis Vuitton. Classy
...dbags and accessories are the
...nstays and prices can be jaw-
...pingly high. (☑91 426 35 88; Calle
...rrano 26 & 34; ⊙10am-8.30pm Mon-
...Ⓜ Serrano)

...ntequería Bravo
FOOD, WINE

 Map p90, B5

...nd the attractive old facade lies
...nnoisseur's paradise, filled with

 Top Tip

Opening Hours
Most of the shops along Calle de
José Ortega y Gasset, and many
other fashion boutiques dotted
around the *barrio*, open from 10am
to 8.30pm Monday to Saturday.

local cheeses, sausages, wines and
coffees. Not that long ago, Mantequería Bravo won the prize for Madrid's
best gourmet food shop or delicatessen. (Calle de Ayala 24; ⊙9.30am-2.30pm
& 5.30-8.30pm Mon-Fri, 9.30am-2.30pm Sat;
Ⓜ Serrano)

Purificación García

24 Map p90, B6

Fashions may come and go but Puri
consistently manages to keep ahead
of the pack. Her signature style for
men and women encompasses elegant
and mature designs that are just as at
home in the workplace as at a wedding. (☑91 435 80 13; www.purificacion
garcia.com; Calle de Serrano 28; ⊙10am-
8.30pm Mon-Sat; Ⓜ Serrano)

Top Sights
Plaza de Toros & Museo Taurino

Getting There

Ⓜ Metro Las Ventas
Metro station (line 2)
sits right outside the
bullring – getting there
couldn't be easier.

East of central Madrid, the Plaza de Toros Monumental de Las Ventas (often known simply as La
Ventas) is the heart and soul of Spain's bullfighting tradition and, as such, is the most important
bullring in the world. To be carried high on the
shoulders of aficionados out through the Puerta de
Madrid is the ultimate dream of any *torero* (bull-
fighter) – if you've made it at Las Ventas, you've
reached the pinnacle of the bullfighting world.

Facade of Las Ventas

Calle de Alcalá 237

M Las Ventas

n't Miss

hitecture

of the largest rings in the bullfighting
d, Las Ventas has a grand Mudéjar (a Moor-
architectural style) exterior and a suitably
osseum–like arena surrounding the broad
ly ring. It was opened in 1931 and hosted its
fight three years later; its four storeys can
25,000 spectators.

rta de Madrid

grand and decidedly Moorish Puerta de Ma-
symbolises the aspiration of all bullfighters
suitably, it's known colloquially as the 'Gate
lory'. Madrid's bullfighting crowd is known
e most demanding in Spain – if they carry a
ro out through the gate (usually clutching an
or a tale – trophies only awarded to an elite
, it's because he has performed exceptionally.

ded Tours

ded visits (conducted in English and Span-
take you out onto the sand and into the
l box; they last 40 minutes and start on the
r. For reservations, contact **Las Ventas Tour**
87 739 032; www.lasventastour.com; adult/child
; ☺10am-6pm, days of bullfight 10am-2pm). The
s are a terrific way to get a feel for the whole
erience.

seo Taurino

ain some insight into the whole subculture
surrounds bullfighting, wander into the Mu-
Taurino. Here you'll find a curious collection
araphernalia, costumes (the *traje de luces*, or
of lights, is one of bullfighting's most recog-
ble props), photos and other bullfighting
norabilia up on the top floor above one of the
courtyards by the ring.

Bullfighting Facts

▶ The bullfighting sea-
son runs from around
the Fiestas de San
Isidro in early May (daily
bullfights) through to
October (weekends
only).

▶ Bullfighting's popular-
ity is waning in Madrid
and the average age
of paying spectators
increases with each
passing year.

▶ Even so, bullfights
during Madrid's Fiesta
de San Isidro remain
hugely popular and a
Barcelona-style ban is
extremely unlikely.

Explore

Malasaña & Chueca

Malasaña and Chueca are where Madrid gets up close and personal.
Yes, there are rewarding museums and examples of landmark architecture sprinkled throughout. But these two inner-city *barrios* are
more about doing than seeing. Here, it's more the experience of life
as it's lived by *madrileños* than the traditional traveller experience
ticking off a list of attractions.

e Sights in a Day

Start with a coffee (or perhaps *chocolate con churros*) at **Café nercial** (p109), just as writers and lectuals have done for decades. down the hill to Plaza Dos de o, a lovely square that's quiet by and busy by night – very Malasaña. for a coffee at **Café Manuela** 9) or **Lolina Vintage Café** (p103) oth!), then window-shop for retro at the **Mercado de Fuencarral** 2). For lunch, take your pick be- en **Nina** (p107), **La Musa** (p106) or **ır** (p107).

After lunch wander down into Chueca, pausing to admire **Sociedad General de Autores y ores** (p106), before visiting the **seo de Historia** (p106). Catch the surrounding Madrid's reconceived kets at the **Mercado de San Antón** 8), then find out what Chueca's all ut at **Diurno** (p111).

Gay Chueca eases into the night at **Café Acuarela** (p109), while as crawl for dinner could take in **aito** (p108). Storied cocktail bars und, but none rival world-famous **eo Chicote** (p109). **La Vía Láctea** 3) is very Malasaña, whereafter we **El Junco Jazz Club** (p111) to see rough until dawn.

a local's day in Malasaña, see p102.

🔍 Local Life

Counterculture in Malasaña (p102)

💗 Best of Malasaña & Chueca

Retro Fashions
Mercado de Fuencarral (p102)

Snapo (p113)

El Templo de Susu (p113)

Gay Chueca
Café Acuarela (p109)

Why Not? (p112)

Black & White (p112)

Cocktail Bars
Museo Chicote (p109)

Del Diego (p111)

Getting There

Ⓜ **Metro** For Malasaña, the best stations are Bilbao (lines 1 and 4), Tribunal (lines 1 and 10), San Bernardo (2 and 4) and Noviciado (2). Chueca station (line 5) is in the heart of the *barrio* of the same name, while Alonso Mar- tínez (4, 5 and 10) can be useful. Gran Vía (1 and 5) is good for both Malasaña and Chueca.

Local Life
Counterculture in Malasaña

Malasaña was the epicentre of *la movida madrileña* in the 1980s and that spirit lives on here. Partly it survives in retro bars, nightclubs and shops that pay homage to the '70s and '80s. But there's also a 'new' and appealing trend towards the vintage aspect of Malasaña life. The common theme is the alternative slant these places take on life in their bid to relive or re-create the past.

❶ Mercado de Fuencarral

Madrid's home of alternative club co
Mercado de Fuencarral (www.mdf.es; C
de Fuencarral 45; 🕙11am-9pm Mon-Sat; M
bunal) is still going strong, revelling i
reverse snobbery. With shops like Fu
Ugly Shop and Black Kiss, it's funky
grungy and filled to the rafters with
torn T-shirts and more black leather
and silver studs than you'll ever nee
When it was threatened with closure
2008 there was nearly an uprising.

Retro City

..asaña down to its Dr Martens,
..ro City (Calle de la Corredera Alta de
.. Pablo 4; ⏱11.30am-9pm Mon-Thu,
..n-9.30pm Fri & Sat; Ⓜ Tribunal), with its
..tage for the masses', lives for the
..urful '70s and '80s. Whereas other
..es in the *barrio* have gone for an
..ry, thumb-your-nose-at-society
..k, Retro City just looks back with
..talgia.

Lolina Vintage Café

..ina Vintage Café (Calle del Espíritu San-
.., ⏱9am-2.30am Mon-Fri, 10am-2.30am
.. 11am-2.30am Sun; Ⓜ Tribunal) seems to
..e captured the essence of the *bar-
.. in one small space. With a studied
..ro look (comfy old-style chairs and
..as, gilded mirrors and 1970s-era
..llpaper), it confirms that the new
..lasaña is not unlike the old.

Casa Julio

..ity-wide poll for Madrid's best
..*quetas* (croquettes; fried rolls with
..ng) would see half of those polled
..ng for **Casa Julio** (☎91 522 72 74; www
..casajulio.com; Calle de la Madera 37; 6/12
..quetas €5/10; ⏱lunch & dinner Mon-Sat;
..ribunal) and the remainder not do-
..so because they haven't been yet.
..re's the traditional *jamón* (ham)
..iety or more creative choices.

Bar Palentino

..mica tables, not a single attention
..detail, and yet...**Bar Palentino** (☎91
.. 30 58; Calle del Pez 8; bocadillos €1.80-
..); ⏱7am-2pm Mon-Sat; Ⓜ Noviciado) is

an ageless Malasaña bar wildly popular
with young and old alike. Its irresist-
ible charm derives from its tables, and
owners María Dolores (she claims to be
'the house speciality') and Casto.

❻ Tupperware

A Malasaña stalwart and prime
candidate for the bar that best
catches the enduring *rockero* spirit of
Malasaña, **Tupperware** (☎91 446 42 04;
Calle de la Corredera Alta de San Pablo 26;
⏱8pm-3.30am Tue-Sat; Ⓜ Tribunal) draws
a thirty-something crowd, spins indie
rock with a bit of soul and classics
from the '60s and '70s, and generally
revels in its kitsch.

❼ La Vía Láctea

A living, breathing and delightfully
grungy relic of *la movida*, **La Vía
Láctea** (Calle de Velarde 18; ⏱9pm-3am;
Ⓜ Tribunal) remains a Malasaña favourite for an informal crowd who lives
for the 1980s. The music ranges from
rock, pop, garage, rockabilly and indie.
Expect long queues on weekends.

❽ Nasti Club

The graffiti and abandoned building
look of **Nasti Club** (☎91 521 76 05; www
.nasti.es; Calle de San Vicente Ferrer 33;
admission free-€10; ⏱10pm-6am Thu-Sat;
Ⓜ Tribunal) marks this out as a place
with attitude. As its own public-
ity says, it is not from Barcelona, it
doesn't play electronica, and no one's
ever heard of the live acts who appear
here until they become famous two
years later. Very Malasaña.

A **B** **C** **D**

C de Alberto Aguilera

San Bernardo

Glorieta
de Ruiz
Jiménez

C de Carranz

1

C de Santa Cruz de Maroenado

C del Conde Duque

C de los Mártires de Alcalá

C de Manuela Malasaña ⊗5

⊗7

Museo
Municipal de Arte
Contemporáneo
⊙2 **CONDE DUQUE**

C de Montserrat

C del Divino Pastor

C de San Bernardo

C de Ruiz

C de San Andrés

Plaza
Guardias
de Corps

C de Quiñones

Plaza
del Dos de
Mayo

C de San Bernardo

C de Daoiz

C de Bernardo López García

2 Ⓜ
Ventura
Rodríguez

Ⓜ C de la Princesa

Travesía del Conde Duque

C del Acuerdo

C de Norte

C de la Palma

MALASAÑA

C de San Bernardino

C del Noviciado

C de San Vicente Ferrer

15 C c
⊙

C de Amaniel

C del Espíritu Santo

Plaza del
Juan Pujol

Noviciado Ⓜ

C del Tesoro

3

Plaza de
Emilio Jiménez
Millas

C del Maestro Guerrero

Noviciado Ⓜ

C de la Marqués de Santa Ana

C de Dc
Felipe

C de Jesús del Valle

Plaza
de España

C de los Reyes

C de Andrés Borrego

C del Pez

C de San Bernardo

C de Pizarro

C de la Madera

C del Molin

Plaza
de España

**Cuesta de
San Vicente**

C de Antonio
Grilo

C de San Roque

C de la Corredera Baja de

C Parada

C de la Luna

C del Río

C de la Corredera

C de

C del Reloj

C de Leganitos

C de Fomento

C de la
Flor Alta

C de Silva

C del Loreto
y Chicote

C del Desengan

4

Jardines
de Sabatini

Ⓒ C de Bailén

Plaza de
la Marina
Española

C de Torija

Santo
Domingo

C de Tudescos

Plaza de
la Encarnación

C de la Bola

Santo
Domingo

Plaza de
Santo
Domingo

**Plaza
del
Callao**

Gran Vía

C de la Abada

C de San Quintín

Ⓜ Santo Domingo

Callao Ⓜ

C de Preciados

C de l

5

Jardines
Cabo
Naval

C de Campomanes

Santo
Domingo

C del Carmen

Pla
Ca

Palacio
Real

C de Felipe V

C de Arrieta

C de Conchas

Plaza de
San Martín

Plaza
de Isabel II

Plaza
de las
Descalzas

Plaza
de
Oriente

C de Francisco Rojas
C de Manuel Silvela
C de Nicasio Gallego
C de Eguilaz
C de José Marañón
C de Manuel González Longoria
C de Almagro
C de Santa Engracia

C de Sagasta
C de Larra
C Serrano Anguita
C de Melía Lequerica
Plaza de Alonso Martínez
Alonso Martínez
Alonso Martínez
C de Zurbano
C de Fernando el Santo

de Apodaca
C de Barceló
Plaza de Santa Bárbara
C de Orfila
C de Alcalá Galiano

Museo de Historia
1
C de la Beneficencia
C de San Mateo
26
C de Hortaleza
21
C de Campoamor
C de Génova
C de Orellana
Plaza de la Villa de París
Paseo de la Castellana

Jardines Arquitecto Rivera
C de San Lorenzo
3
Sociedad General de Autores y Editores
C de Argensola
C del General Castaños
Plaza de Colón

ón
C de la Santa Brígida
C de la Farmacia
C de Palayo
C de Belén
Plaza de las Salesas
C del Marqués de la Ensenada

C de Hernán Cortés
C de Gravina
CHUECA
C San Lucas
C de Piamonte
C de Bárbara de Braganza
18

C de Augusto Figueroa
14
Chueca
23
C del Conde de Xiquena
C del Almirante
Galería Moriarty
4

C de Hortaleza
C de San Marcos
22
C de Barbieri
C de la Libertad
C de Tamayo y Baus
C de Prim
19

10
20
C de Barquillo
Paseo de los Recoletos
C del Cid

9
Plaza del Rey
C de Salustiano

Vía de is
C de Clavel
C de la Reina
11
C de las Infantas
Paseo del Prado
Banco de España

16
13
C del Caballero de Gracia
Gran Vía
C de Alcalá

Jardines
a Aduana
Sevilla
Banco de España

For reviews see	
◉ Sights	p106
✕ Eating	p106
☻ Drinking	p109
✪ Entertainment	p111
🔒 Shopping	p113

Sights

Museo de Historia
MUSEUM

1 Map p104, E2

The fine Museo de Historia (formerly the Museo Municipal) has an elaborate and restored baroque entrance, raised in 1721 by Pedro de Ribera. The interior is dominated by paintings and other memorabilia charting the historical evolution of Madrid, of which the highlight is Goya's *Allegory of the City of Madrid*. Also worth lingering over is the expansive model of 1830s Madrid. (www.munimadrid.es/museodehistoria; Calle de Fuencarral 78; admission free; ⏱9.30am-8pm Tue-Fri, 10am-2pm Sat & Sun; Ⓜ Tribunal)

Museo Municipal de Arte Contemporáneo
MUSEUM

2 Map p104, B2

Spread over two floors, this is a rich collection of modern Spanish art, mostly paintings and graphic art with a smattering of photography, sculpture and drawings. The museum was closed for major renovations at the time of writing with no scheduled date for reopening. (📞91 588 59 28; www.munimadrid.es/museoartecontemporaneo; Calle del Conde Duque 9-11; admission free; Ⓜ Plaza de España, Ventura Rodríguez, San Bernardo)

Sociedad General de Autores y Editores
ARCHITECT

3 Map p104, F3

This swirling, melting wedding cake of a building is as close as Madrid comes to the work of Antoni Gaudí, which so illuminates Barcelona. It's a joyously self-indulgent ode to *modernismo* and is virtually one of a kind in Madrid. Casual visitors are actively discouraged, although what you see from the street is impressive enough. (General Society of Authors & Editors; Calle Fernando VI 4; Ⓜ Alonso Martínez)

Galería Moriarty
GALL

4 Map p104, G3

During *la movida madrileña* in the 1980s, Galería Moriarty (then in Ca del Almirante) was one of Madrid's most important meeting places of c ture and counterculture, drawing th icons of the day to its exhibitions ar parties. It remains one of the most important small galleries in Madrid (📞91 531 43 65; www.galeriamoriarty.com Calle de Tamayo y Baus 6; ⏱11am-2pm & 5-8.30pm Tue-Sat; Ⓜ Chueca, Colón)

Eating

La Musa
SPANISH, FUSION

5 Map p104, D1

Snug yet loud, a favourite of Madri hip young crowd yet utterly unprete tious, La Musa is all about designer

 pas and sangria

or, lounge music on the sound
tem and food (breakfast, lunch
d dinner) that will live long in the
mory and is always fun and filled
h flavour. The menu is divided
o three types of tapas – hot, cold
l BBQ. It doesn't take reservations.
91 448 75 58; www.lamusa.com.es; Calle
Manuela Malasaña 18; mains €7-15; 9am-
-Mon-Thu, 9am-2am Fri, 1pm-2am Sat,
-1am Sun; San Bernardo)

na   CONTEMPORARY SPANISH €€

Map p104, D1

histicated, intimate and endur-
ly popular, Nina has an extensive
nu of Mediterranean nouvelle
sine that doesn't miss a trick. We

like the decor, all exposed brick and
subtle lighting, and we love just about
everything on the menu. The weekend
brunch is excellent. (91 591 00 46;
Calle de Manuela Malasaña 10; mains €11.50-
16; lunch & dinner; Bilbao)

Albur   TAPAS, SPANISH €€

7 Map p104, D1

One of Malasaña's best deals, this
place has a wildly popular tapas bar
and a classy but casual restaurant
out the back. Albur is known for terrific rice dishes and tapas, and has a
well-chosen wine list. (91 594 27 33;
www.restaurantealbur.com; Calle de Manuela
Malasaña 15; mains €13-18; noon-1am Sun-
Thu, noon-2am Fri & Sat; Bilbao)

Top Tip

Two Dinner Sittings

In order to make the most of their popularity, some restaurants in Malasaña and elsewhere offer two sittings on Friday and Saturday nights, usually around 9pm and 11pm. Unless you can't wait, we recommend reserving a table for the second sitting – otherwise you'll often get the feeling that they're trying to hurry you along.

Bodega de la Ardosa

TAPAS €

 8   Map p104, E3

Going strong since 1892, the charming, wood-panelled bar of Bodega de la Ardosa could equally be recommended as a favourite Malasaña drinking hole. Then again, to come here and not try the *salmorejo* (cold, tomato-based soup), *croquetas* (croquettes), *patatas bravas* (fried potatoes with spicy tomato sauce) or *tortilla de patatas* (potato omelette) would be a crime. (☑91 521 49 79; Calle de Colón 13; tapas & raciones €3.50-11; ⊘8.30am-1am; ⓂTribunal)

Bocaito

TAPAS €€

 9   Map p104, F4

Film-maker Pedro Almodóvar once described this traditional bar and restaurant as 'the best antidepressant'. Jam into the bar shoulder to shoulder with the casual crowd, order one of the specialties (mussels with bechamel, canapes and fried fish) and enjoy the theatre in which these busy barstaff excel. (☑91 532 12 19; www.bocaito.com; Calle de la Libertad 4-6; tapas from €3.50, mains €12-20; ⊘lunch & dinner Mon-Fri, dinner Sat; ⓂChueca, Banco de España)

Mercado de San Antón

TAPAS

 10   Map p104, F4

On the first floor of this busy Chueca market is a range of fine tapas bars where the cuisine spans Japanese, Italian and Greek with some wonderful Spanish options – Stall 23 has some fabulous tapas. (www.mercadosananton.com; Calle de Augusto Figueroa 24; meals €10-30; ⊘10am-midnight Mon-Thu, 10am-1.30am Fri-Sun; ⓂChueca)

La Paella de la Reina

MEDITERRANEAN

 11   Map p104, F5

Madrid is not renowned for its paella (Valencia is king in that regard), but Valencianos who can't make it home are known to frequent La Paella de la Reina. Like any decent paella restaurant, you need two people to make an order but, that requirement satisfied, you've plenty of choice. The typical Valencia paella is cooked with beans, chicken and rabbit, but there are also plenty of seafood varieties on offer, including *arroz negro* (black rice whose colour derives from squid ink). (☑91 531 18 85; www.lapaelladelareina.com; Calle de la Reina 39; mains €13.90-24; ⓂBanco de España)

rinking

fé Comercial
CAFE

 Map p104, E1

s glorious old Madrid cafe proudly
ts a rearguard action against
gress with heavy leather seats,
ndant marble and old-style waiters.
é Comercial, which dates back to
7, is the largest of the *barrio's* old
es and has changed little since those
s, although the clientele has broad-
d to include just about anyone,
m writers on their laptops to old
playing chess. (Glorieta de Bilbao 7;
30am-midnight Mon-Thu, 7.30am-2am Fri,
0am-2am Sat, 9am-midnight Sun; MBilbao)

seo Chicote
COCKTAIL BAR

 Map p104, F5

e founder of this Madrid landmark
aid to have invented more than a
ndred cocktails, which the likes of
mingway, Ava Gardner, Grace Kelly,
hia Loren and Frank Sinatra all
oyed at one time or another. It's still
quented by film stars and socialites,
it's at its best after midnight,
en a lounge atmosphere takes over,
ples cuddle on the curved benches
l some of the city's best DJs do their
ff. (www.museo-chicote.com; Gran Vía 12;
5pm-3am Mon-Thu, 6pm-4am Fri & Sat;
Gran Vía)

Café Acuarela
CAFE, GAY

14 Map p104, F3

A few steps up the hill from Plaza
de Chueca and long a centrepiece of
gay Madrid – a huge statue of a nude
male angel guards the doorway –
this is an agreeable, dimly lit salon
decorated with, among other things,
religious icons! It's ideal for quiet
conversation and catching the weekend buzz as people plan their forays
into the more clamorous clubs in the
vicinity. (www.cafeacuarela.es; Calle de
Gravina 10; 11am-2am Sun-Thu, to 3am Fri
& Sat; MChueca)

Café Manuela
CAFE

15 Map p104, D2

Stumbling into this graciously restored throwback to the 1950s along
one of Malasaña's grittier streets is
akin to discovering hidden treasure.
There's a luminous quality to it when
you come in out of the night and, like
so many Madrid cafes, it's a surprisingly multifaceted space, serving
cocktails, delicious milkshakes and
offering board games atop the marble
tables in the unlikely event that you
get bored. (Calle de San Vicente Ferrer 29;
9am-2am Mon-Fri, 10am-3am Sat, 10am-
2am Sun; MTribunal)

Understand

La Movida Madrileña

What London was to the swinging '60s and Paris to 1968, Madrid was to the 1980s. After the long years of dictatorship and conservative Catholicism, the death of Franco and the advent of democracy, Spaniards, especially *madrileños*, were prompted to emerge onto the streets with all the zeal of ex-convent schoolgirls. Nothing was taboo in a phenomenon known as *la movida madrileña* (literally the Madrid scene) as young *madrileños* discovered the '60s, '70s and '80s all at once. Drinking, drugs and sex suddenly were OK. All-night partying was the norm, drug taking in public was not a criminal offence (that changed in 1992) and the city howled.

What was remarkable about *la movida* was that it was presided over by Enrique Tierno Galván, an ageing, former university professor who had been a leading opposition figure under Franco and was affectionately known throughout Spain as 'the old teacher'. A Socialist, he became mayor in 1979 and, for many, launched *la movida* by telling a public gathering '*a colocarse y ponerse al loro*', which loosely translates as 'get stoned and do what's cool'. Unsurprisingly he was Madrid's most popular mayor ever and when he died in 1986 a million *madrileños* turned out for his funeral.

La movida was not just about rediscovering the Spanish art of *salir de copas* ('going out for a drink'). It was also accompanied by an explosion of creativity among the country's musicians, designers and film-makers keen to shake off the shackles of the Franco years. By one tally, Madrid was home to 300 rock bands and 1500 fashion designers during *la movida*. The most famous of these was film director Pedro Almodóvar. Although his later films became internationally renowned, his first films, *Pepi, Luci, Bom y Otras Chicas del Montón* (1980) and *Laberinto de Pasiones* (1982) are where the spirit of the movement really comes alive.

At the height of *la movida* in 1981, Andy Warhol openly regretted that he could not spend the rest of his days here. In 1985, the *New York Times* anointed the Spanish capital 'the new cultural capital of the world and the place to be'. Things have quietened down a little since those heady days, but you'll only notice if you were here during the 1980s...

l Diego
COCKTAIL BAR

⊙ Map p104, E5

...e de la Reina is much loved by
...osos, especially models, actors
...d designers, as a place for terrific
...ktails in stately surrounds. Del
...go fits this bill perfectly and dur-
...its 20 years of existence has
...ome one of the city's most cel-
...ated cocktail bars. (☎91 523 31 06;
...e de la Reina 12; ⊙7pm-3am Mon-Thu,
...-3.30am Fri & Sat; ⓜGran Vía)

...fé Pepe Botella
CAFE, BAR

⊙ Map p104, D2

...e Botella has hit on a fine formula
...success. As good in the hours
...und midnight as it is in the after-
...n when its wi-fi access draws the
...top-toting crowd, it's a classy bar
...h green-velvet benches, marble-
...ped tables and old photos and
...rors covering the walls. (Calle de
...Andrés 12; ⊙10am-2am Mon-Thu, 10am-
...am Fri & Sat, 11am-2am Sun; ⓜBilbao,
...unal)

...fé-Restaurante ...Espejo
CAFE

⊙ Map p104, H3

...e a haunt of writers and intel-
...tuals, this architectural gem blends
...dern and art deco styles, while its
...erior could well overwhelm you
...h all the mirrors, chandeliers and
...v-tied service of another era. (Paseo
...os Recoletos 31; ⊙8am-midnight Sun-Thu,
...m-3am Fri & Sat; ⓜColón)

Gran Café de Gijón
CAFE

19 ⊙ Map p104, H4

This graceful old cafe has been serving
coffee and meals since 1888 and has
long been a favourite with Madrid's
literati for a drink or a meal. You'll
find yourself among intellectuals,
conservative Franco diehards and
young *madrileños* looking for a quiet
drink. (www.cafegijon.com; Paseo de los
Recoletos 21; ⊙7am-1.30am; ⓜChueca,
Banco de España)

Diurno
CAFE

20 ⊙ Map p104, F4

One of the most important hubs of
barrio life in Chueca, this cafe (with
DVD store attached) has become
to modern Chueca what the grand
literary cafes were to another age. It's
always full with a fun Chueca crowd
relaxing amid the greenery. They also
serve well-priced meals and snacks
if you can't bear to give up your seat.
(www.diurno.com; Calle de San Marcos 37;
⊙9am-midnight Mon-Thu, 9am-1am Fri, 10am-
1am Sat, 10am-midnight Sun; ⓜChueca)

Entertainment

El Junco Jazz Club
JAZZ, CLUB

21 ☆ Map p104, F2

El Junco has established itself on the
Madrid nightlife scene by appealing
as much to jazz aficionados as to club-
bers. Its secret is high-quality, live jazz
gigs from Spain and around the world,

Tupperware bar (p103)

followed by DJs spinning funk, soul, nu jazz, blues and innovative groove beats. (☎91 319 20 81; www.eljunco.com; Plaza de Santa Bárbara 10; concerts €6-10; ⏰8pm-3.30pm Mon, 8pm-6am Tue-Fri, 11pm-6am Sat & Sun, concerts 11pm Tue-Sun; Ⓜ Alonso Martínez)

Why Not?

CLUB

23 ⭐ Map p104, F4

Underground, narrow and packed with bodies, gay-friendly Why Not? is the sort of place where nothing's left to the imagination. Pop and top 40 music are the standard here, and the dancing crowd is mixed and as serious about having a good time as they are about heavy petting. (www.whynotmad .com; Calle de San Bartolomé 7; admission €10; ⏰10.30pm-6am; Ⓜ Chueca)

Black & White

GAY, C

23 ⭐ Map p104, F4

People still talk about the opening party of Black & White way back in 1982 and ever since, it has been a pioneer of Chueca's gay nights. This place is extravagantly gay with drag acts, male strippers and a refreshin no-holds-barred approach to life. (w .discoblack-white.net; Calle de la Libertad 3 ⏰10pm-5.30am Sun-Thu, 10pm-6am Fri & Sat; Ⓜ Chueca)

hopping

dolfo Domínguez FASHION

4 🔒 Map p104, E4

e stylish shop of this inventive
anish designer is where you'll find
erly casual and colourful designs
the consciously cool among us.
91 523 39 38; www.adolfodominguez.com;
le de Fuencarral 5; ⏲10am-9pm Mon-Sat;
Gran Vía)

usto Barcelona FASHION

5 🔒 Map p104, E4

e chic shop of Barcelona designer
sto Dalmau wears its Calle de
encarral address well, because the
nic T-shirts are at once edgy, awash
attitude and artfully displayed. It's
t to everyone's taste, but always
rth a look. (☎91 360 46 36; www.custo
rcelona.com; Calle de Fuencarral 29;
10am-9pm Mon-Sat, noon-8pm Sun;
Gran Vía)

atrimonio Comunal
livarero FOOD

6 🔒 Map p104, F2

catch the real essence of the coun-
's olive oil varieties (Spain is the
rld's largest producer), Patrimonio
munal Olivarero is perfect. With
amples of the extra virgin variety
nd nothing else) from all over Spain,
u could spend ages agonising over
e choices. (www.pco.es; Calle de Mejía
querica 1; ⏲10am-2pm & 5-8pm Mon-Fri,
am-2pm Sat; MAlonso Martínez)

☑ Top Tip

Opening Hours

Although they don't advertise
it in their opening hours, many
shops along Calle de Fuencarral
also open on Sundays. Your best
chance is usually the first Sunday
of the month.

Snapo CLOTHING, ACCESSORIES

27 🔒 Map p104, D3

Snapo is rebellious Malasaña to its
core, thumbing its nose at the niceties
of fashion respectability. It does jeans,
caps and jackets, but its T-shirts are
the Snapo trademark. Down through
the years, we've seen everything
from a mocked-up cover of 'National
Pornographic' to Pope John Paul II
with fist raised and 'Vatican 666'
emblazoned across the front. Need we
say more? (☎91 532 12 23; Calle del Espíritu
Santo 5; ⏲11am-2pm & 5-8.30pm Mon-Sat;
MTribunal)

El Templo de
Susu CLOTHING, ACCESSORIES

28 🔒 Map p104, D3

It won't appeal to everyone, but El
Templo de Susu's secondhand clothes
from the 1960s and 1970s have clearly
found a market. It's kind of like char-
ity shop meets unreconstructed
hippie, which is either truly awful or
retro cool, depending on your perspec-
tive. (☎91 523 31 22; Calle del Espíritu Santo
1; ⏲11am-9pm Mon-Sat; MTribunal)

Top Sights
Ermita de San Antonio de la Florida

Getting There

Ⓜ **Metro** Go to Príncipe Pío station (lines 6 and 10). The Ermita de San Antonio de la Florida is the southern of two chapels, a 500m walk northwest along the Paseo de la Florida.

From the outside, this humble hermitage gives no hint of the splendour that lies within. But make no mistake, this small church ranks alongside Madrid's finest art galleries on the list of must-sees for art lovers. Recently restored and also known as the Panteón de Goya, this chapel has frescoed ceilings painted by Goya in 1798 on the request of Carlos IV. As such, it's one of the few places to see Goya masterworks in their original setting.

Goya artwork, Ermita de San Antonio de la Florida

on't Miss

e Miracle of St Anthony

gures on the dome depict the miracle of St
thony. The saint heard word from his native
sbon that his father had been unjustly accused
murder. The saint was whisked miraculously
his hometown from northern Italy and Goya's
inting depicts the moment in which St Anthony
ls on the corpse to rise up and absolve his
her.

18th-Century Madrid Crowd

interesting as the miracle that forms the fres-
es' centrepiece, a typical Madrid crowd swarms
ound the saint. It was customary in such works
at angels and cherubs appear in the cupola,
ove all the terrestrial activity, but Goya, never
e to let himself be confined within the mores
the day, places the human above the divine.

ya's Tomb

e painter is buried in front of the altar. His
mains were transferred in 1919 from Bordeaux
rance), where he had died in self-imposed exile
1828. Oddly, the skeleton that was exhumed in
rdeaux was missing one important item – the
ad.

earby: Templo de Debod

the hill from the Ermita, this Egyptian **temple**
ww.munimadrid.es/templodebod; Paseo del Pintor
sales; admission free; ⏱10am-2pm & 6-8pm Tue-Fri,
am-2pm Sat & Sun; Ⓜ Ventura Rodríguez) was saved
m the rising waters of Lake Nasser (Egypt)
ring the building of the Aswan Dam. After 1968
was sent block by block to Spain as a gesture of
anks to Spanish archaeologists in the Unesco
am that worked to save the monuments.

Glorieta de San
Antonio de la Florida 5

admission free

⏱9.30am-8pm Tue-Fri,
10am-2pm Sat & Sun,
hours vary Jul & Aug

Ⓜ Príncipe Pío

☑ Top Tips

▸ Check the opening
hours as these do vary
from the official hours.
This is particularly the
case in July & August.

▸ On 13 June every year
it's a Madrid tradition
for seamstresses to
come here to pray for
a partner, although the
tradition now extends to
young women from all
walks of life.

✕ Take a Break

Casa Mingo (☎91 547 79
18; www.casamingo.es;
Paseo de la Florida 34;
raciones €3.95-10.30;
⏱lunch & dinner; Ⓜ Prínc-
ipe Pío), next to the
Ermita, is a well-known
Asturian cider house. It
focuses primarily on its
signature dish of *pollo
asado* (roast chicken)
accompanied by a
bottle of cider.

Local Life
Barrio Life in Chamberí

Getting There

Chamberí is well-connected to the rest of Madrid.

Ⓜ **Metro** Quevedo (line 2), Bilbao (lines 1 and 4) and Iglesia (line 1) stations all set you up nicely for a visit to the area.

The generally upmarket *barrio* of Chamberí is widely known as one of the most *castizo* (a difficu term to translate, its meaning lies somewhere be-tween traditional and authentic) neighbourhoods the capital. With its signature plaza, old-style sho and unmistakeable *barrio* feel, it's one of Madrid' best places to understand what makes the city tic away from well-worn tourist trails.

Plaza de Olavide

za de Olavide is the hub of
amberí life with its park benches,
ygrounds and outdoor tables. In-
e Bar Mentrida at No 3 you'll find
irring photographic record of the
za's history.

Old-Fashioned Shopping

harming old-world shoe store,
zados Cantero (✆91 447 07 35; Plaza de
vide 12; ✆10am-2pm & 4.45-8.30pm Mon-
MQuevedo, Iglesia, Bilbao) are famous
their rope-soled *alpargatas* (espa-
lles), which start from €6. This place
barrio classic, the sort of place that
ents bring their children as their
n parents did a generation before.

Antique Fans

e tiny shop of **Antigüedades Hom**
91 594 20 17; Calle de Juan de Austria 31;
-8pm Mon-Wed, noon-2pm & 5-8pm Thu
ri; MIglesia) specialises in delicately
dpainted fans and those made
h bone. It opens afternoons only
ause the owner spends the morn-
restoring the fans you see for sale.

A Surprise Museum

wn the bottom end of Chamberí,
seo Sorolla (http://museosorolla.mcu
Paseo del General Martínez Campos 37;
lt/child €3/free, free Sun; ✆9.30am-8pm
-Sat, 10am-3pm Sun; MIglesia, Gregorio
añón) is one of Madrid's best-kept
rets. Dedicated to the Valencian
st Joaquín Sorolla, who immortal-
d the clear Mediterranean light of
Valencian coast, his Madrid house
tains the most complete collection
he artist's works.

5 A Barrio Bar

Back up the hill into the heart of
Chamberí, **Bodega de la Ardosa** (✆91
446 58 94; Calle de Santa Engracia 70; raciones from €6.50; ✆9am-3pm & 6-11.30pm
Thu-Tue; MIglesia) is a fine old relic with
an extravagantly tiled facade. Locals
prop up the bar and come for some of
the best traditional Spanish *patatas
bravas* (fried potatoes with a spicy
tomato sauce) in town.

6 Chamberí's Missing Station

For years, *madrileños* wondered what
happened to their metro station.
Abandoned in 1966, **Estación de
Chamberí** (Andén 0; www.esmadrid.com/
anden0/; cnr Calles de Santa Engracia & de
Luchana; admission free; ✆11am-7pm Tue-Fri,
11am-3pm Sat & Sun; MIglesia, Bilbao) has
finally reopened as a museum piece
that re-creates the era of the station's
inauguration in 1919, with memorabilia almost a century old.

7 Calle de Fuencarral

Calle de Fuencarral between the
Glorietas de Bilbao and Quevedo is
one of Madrid's iconic thoroughfares.
On Sunday mornings, the street is
closed to traffic from 8am to 2pm.

8 Basque Tapas

At journey's end, **Sagaretxe** (✆91 446
25 88; www.sagaretxe.com; Calle de Eloy
Gonzalo 26; tapas from €2.50; ✆noon-5pm
& 7pm-1am; MIglesia), just around the
corner from where you started, is one
of the best Basque *pintxos* (tapas)
bars in Madrid. Simply point and your
selection will be plated up for you.

Top Sights
San Lorenzo de El Escorial

Getting There

🚆 **Train** A few dozen Renfe C8 *cercanías* (local train network) trains make the one-hour trip daily from Madrid's Atocha or Chamartín stations to El Escorial.

🚌 **Bus** Take bus 661 or 664 from Madrid's Moncloa Intercambiador de Autobuses.

Home to the majestic monastery and palace complex of San Lorenzo de El Escorial, this one-time royal getaway rises up from the foothills of the mountains that shelter Madrid from the north and west. The prim little town is overflowing with quaint shops, restaurants and hotels, and the fresh cool air, among other things, has been drawing city dwellers here since the complex was first built on the orders of King Felipe II in the 16th century.

San Lorenzo de El Escorial

on't Miss

torical Background

understanding of El Escorial's historical story
s a long way. For example, as was the royal
rogative in those days, several villages were
n down to make way for the undertaking,
ch included a royal palace and a mausoleum
Felipe's parents, Carlos I and Isabel. Architect
n de Herrera oversaw the project.

st Steps

ist the urge to rush to the heart of the com-
x, and linger over the monastery's main en-
nce on the west side of the complex. Above the
eway a statue of St Lawrence stands watch,
ding a symbolic gridiron, the instrument of
martyrdom (he was roasted alive on one).

tio de los Reyes

er passing St Lawrence and grimacing at his
e, you'll first enter the Patio de los Reyes (Patio
he Kings), which houses the statues of the six
gs of Judah. Admiring these statues, it's dif-
ılt not to marvel at the arrogance of the Span-
royals who saw nothing amiss in comparing
mselves to the great kings of the past.

sílica

ectly ahead of the Patio de los Reyes lies the
nbre basilica. As you enter, look up at the un-
ıal flat vaulting by the choir stalls. Once inside
church proper, turn left to view Benvenuto
lini's white Carrara marble statue of Christ
cified (1576) – it's one of the most underrated
sterpieces of the complex.

Greco

e remainder of the ground floor contains
ious treasures, including some tapestries
l an El Greco painting – impressive as it is,

☎ 91 890 78 18

www.patrimonio
nacional.es

adult/concession
€10/5, guide/audio
guide €7/4, EU citizens
free 5-8pm Wed & Thu

🕐 10am-8pm Apr-Sep,
10am-6pm Oct-Mar,
closed Mon

☑ Top Tips

▶ If possible, avoid
coming here on a
weekend, as the town
and whole complex can
be overwhelmed by day-
trippers from Madrid.

▶ Visit the website www
.patrimonionacional.es
for a wealth of historical
detail on the complex.

▶ The local tourist office
website (www.san
lorenzoturismo.org) is
good for surrounding
attractions if you plan to
make a day of it.

✕ Take a Break

La Cueva (www.meson
lacueva.com), a block
back from the monas-
tery complex, has been
around since 1768 and
remains a bastion of
traditional Castilian
cooking (especially
roasted meats).

it's a far cry from El Greco's dream of decorating the whole complex. He actually came to Spain from Greece in 1577 hoping to get a job decorating El Escorial, although Felipe II rejected him as a court artist.

Two Museums

After wondering at what might have been had El Greco been given a free hand, head downstairs to the northeastern corner of the complex. You pass through the Museo de Arquitectura and the Museo de Pintura. The former tells (in Spanish) the story of how the complex was built, the latter contains 16th- and 17th-century Italian, Spanish and Flemish art.

Up & Down

The route through the monastery takes you upstairs into a gallery known as the Palacio de Felipe II or Palacio de los Austrias. You'll then descend to the 17th-century Panteón de los Reyes (Crypt of the Kings), where almost all Spain's monarchs since Carlos I are interred. Backtracking a little, you're in the Panteón de los Infantes (Crypt of the Princesses).

Salas Capitulares

Stairs lead up from the Patio de los Evangelistas (Patio of the Gospels) to the Salas Capitulares (chapterhouse) in the southeastern corner of the monastery. These bright, airy rooms

San Lorenzo de El Escorial

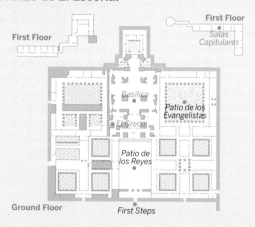

Understand

Developing a Royal Complex

This formidable palace-monastery complex was the brainchild of Spain's King Felipe II (r 1556–1598). Partly conceived as a decadent royal palace and as a mausoleum worthy of Felipe's parents, Carlos I and Isabel, El Escorial was also an announcement to increasingly Protestant Europe that Spain would always be Catholic.

As principal architect, Felipe II chose Juan Bautista de Toledo who had worked on Rome's Basilica of St Peter. The architect's mission was, in the king's words, 'simplicity in the construction, severity in the whole, nobility without arrogance, majesty without ostentation.' In fulfilling these instructions, Juan Bautista de Toledo used locally quarried granite as the primary building material and followed a floor plan based on historical descriptions of Solomon's Temple in Jerusalem.

Several villages were razed to make way for the massive project and the first stone was laid in 1563 (two years after Madrid was chosen as Spain's capital). When Juan Bautista de Toledo died in 1567, architect Juan de Herrera, a towering figure of the Spanish Renaissance, took over the project and saw it through to completion in 1584.

ose ceilings are richly frescoed, tain a treasure chest of works by Greco, Titian, Tintoretto, José de era and Hieronymus Bosch (known El Bosco' to Spaniards).

erta de los Frailes

t south of the monastery is the **erta de los Frailes** (Friars Garden; Oam-7pm Apr-Sep, 10am-6pm Oct-Mar, ed Mon), which merits a stroll. As al gardens go, it's fairly modest, can be a wonderfully tranquil t when the rest of the complex is rming with visitors.

Jardín del Príncipe

The **Prince's Garden** (◷10am-9pm Apr-Sep, 10am-6pm Oct-Mar, closed Mon), which leads down to the town of El Escorial (and the train station), is a lovely monumental garden and contains the **Casita del Príncipe** (guided visits adult/student €3.60/2; ◷10am-8pm Apr-Sep, 10am-6pm Oct-Mar, closed Mon), a little neoclassical gem built in 1772 by Juan de Villanueva under Carlos III for his heir, Carlos IV.

The Best of
Madrid

Madrid's Best Walks

Madrid's Best...

Tapas bar

Best Walks
Architectural Madrid

🏃 The Walk

Madrid may not have the Eiffel Tower, Colosseum or Sagrada Família, but it is easily the rival of Paris, Rome or Barcelona for its astonishing breadth of grand monuments. From the heart of old Madrid to the showpiece architecture of 19th- and 20th-century Spain, this walk takes you through the Spanish capital's splendid architectural attractions. Old Madrid boasts its very own style, while the sometimes bombastic, more often graceful, architectural monuments to the past century cut a swath through the centre of the city and down to the Paseo del Prado, one of Europe's most beautiful boulevards.

Start Plaza de la Villa; **M** Ópera

Finish Antigua Estación de Atocha; **M** Atocha Renfe

Length 5km; two to three hours

✗ Take a Break

Estado Puro (Map p82, A3; 📞 91 330 24 00; www .tapasenestadopuro.com; Plaza de Cánovas del Castillo 4; tapas €5-12.50; 🕚 11am-1am Tue-Sat, 11am-4pm Sun; **M** Banco de España, Atocha)

Palacio de Comunicaciones (p83)

❶ Plaza de la Villa

This compact square (p30) hosts a lovely collection of 17th-century Madrid architecture. The use of brickwork and slate spires are the most distinctive characteristics of a style known as Madrid baroque (*barroco madrileño*).

❷ Plaza de España

Towering over this square on the east side, the **Edificio de España**, which clearly sprang from the totalitarian recesses of Franco imagination such is its resemblance to austere Soviet monumentalism. To the north stands the 35-storey **Torre de Madrid**, another important landmark on the Madrid skyline.

❸ Gran Vía

The iconic **Gran Vía** is defined by towering belle époque facades. Eye-catching buildings include: the Carrión, Madrid's first tower-block apartment hotel; the soaring 1920s-era Telefónica building used for target practice during the Civil War; and the stunning, French-designed Edificio Metrópolis (1905).

Plaza de Cibeles

...drid's most striking ...ndabout (p83) is a ...ring celebration of ...e époque from the ...y 20th century. In ...ition to the **Palacio ...Comunicaciones** ...7), the **Palacio ...Linares**, **Palacio ...enavista** and **Banco ...España** (1891) all ...ch over the square.

Museo del Prado

... building in which ...**Prado** (p66) is ...sed is itself an ar- ...tectural masterpiece. ... western wing was designed by Juan de Villanueva, a towering figure of 18th-century Spanish culture and an architect who left his mark across the capital (eg the Plaza Mayor).

❻ Caixa Forum

Caixa Forum (p83), along the Paseo del Prado, is Madrid's most unusual example of contemporary architecture. Its vertical garden, seeming absence of supporting pillars and wrought-iron roof are unlike anything you'll see elsewhere.

❼ Antigua Estación de Atocha

The northwestern wing of **Atocha train station** was artfully overhauled in 1992. This grand iron and glass relic from the 19th century was preserved while its interior was converted into a light-filled tropical garden. It's a thoroughly modern space that nonetheless resonates with the stately European train stations of another age.

Best Walks
Foodie's Madrid

🏃 The Walk

Food is perhaps the most enduring centrepiece of *madrileño* life, which goes a long way towards explaining why Madrid could just be Spain's most underrated food city. It's to here that all that's good about Spain's culinary traditions and recent decades of innovations have gravitated, and the diversity of culinary experiences on offer is what makes the city such a wonderful introduction to Spanish cuisine. On this walk we begin in one of the country's most innovative food markets, wander down to the world's oldest restaurant, walk the length of one of Spain's best streets for tapas, shop for wines and then partake of a sherry in one of Madrid's classic bars.

Start Mercado de San Miguel; Ⓜ Sol

Finish Lhardy; Ⓜ Sol

Length 2km; two to four hours

✕ Take a Break

Chocolatería de San Ginés (Map p28, D6; Pasadizo de San Ginés 5; 🕘 9.30am-7am; Ⓜ Sol)

Mercado de San Miguel (p32)

❶ Mercado de S Miguel

This wonderfully converted early 20th century market (p32) a gastronome's parad with tapas to be enjo on the spot (everythi from chocolate to caviar), fresh produc every turn and a buz that rarely abates un closing time at 2am. **Casa de Bacalao** (St 17), for example, is a particular favourite.

❷ Casa Revuelta

The decor at **Casa Revuelta** (p32) hasn changed in decades, has the clientele. The come here for the bo less tapas of *bacalao* (cod) and the conviv air of a Madrid bar where the staff shout make themselves hea To understand this city, come here at 1p Sunday.

❸ Restaurante Sobrino de Botín

This is the world's oldest continuously functioning restaura (p32). Roasted meats served in a wonderfu setting (ask for a tab in the vaulted cellar) could easily explain i gevity, but El Botín appears in novels Ernest Hemingway, derick Forsyth and a t of local writers.

Calle de la va Baja

e de la Cava Baja's ledieval streetscape ows the path of Ma-d's long-disappeared ledieval wall. It's also of the great food ets of the world, ne to a slew of as bars that make _atina one of the t places to eat in the ntry.

⑤ María Cabello

There are wine shops where they hand you a catalogue, and then there's **María Cabello** (p63). They know their wines here, and are as at home speaking to experts as to first-timers keen to sample Spanish wines without knowing where to start.

⑥ La Venencia

La Venencia (p58) is the evocation of an old-style Spanish dream. Here they pour the sherry straight from the barrel, they're

not averse to looking grumpy in the honoured tradition of Spanish bartenders and you can almost smell the dust of decades past.

⑦ Lhardy

It'd be a shame to wander around with food on your mind and not wander in here (p56). The ground-floor delicatessen is all about planning a picnic in the Parque del Buen Retiro or buying meats, cheeses and other delicacies to take home. Doing so is _very_ Madrid.

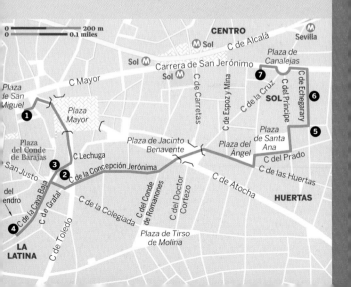

Best
Restaurants

Madrid is arguably the best place to eat in Spain. It's not that the city's culinary traditions are anything to write home about. Rather, everything that is exciting about Spanish cooking has gravitated to the capital, from Basque tapas bars to avant-garde Catalan chefs, from the best in Galician seafood to Andalucía's Mediterranean catch. Travel from one Spanish village to the next and you'll quickly learn that each has its own speciality. Travel to Madrid and you'll find them all.

Madrid Specialties

The city's traditional local cuisine is dominated by hearty stews, particularly in winter, and there are none more hearty than *cocido a la madrileña*, a hotpot or stew that starts with a noodle broth and is followed by, or combined with carrots, chickpeas, chicken, *morcilla* (blood sausage), beef, lard and possibly other sausage meats, too.

Other popular staples in Madrid include *cordero asado* (roast lamb), *croquetas* (croquettes), *patatas con huevos fritos* (baked potatoes with eggs, also known as *huevos rotos*), *tortilla de patatas* (a thick potato omelette) and endless variations on *bacalao* (cod).

Regional Spanish Cuisine

But this is only half the story. Madrid has wholeheartedly embraced dishes – and the innovations that accompany them – from across the country. Most notably, every day tonnes of fish and seafood are trucked in from Mediterranean and Atlantic ports to satisfy the *madrileño* taste for the sea to the extent that, remarkably for a city so far inland, Madrid is home to the world's second-largest fish market (after Tokyo).

Best for Local Cooking

Restaurante Sobrino de Botín The world's oldest restaurant and a hugely atmospheric place to sample roast meats. (p32)

Lhardy The great and the good of Madrid, from royalty to A-list celebrities, have all eaten in this bastion of traditional cooking. (p56)

Taberna La Bola One of the best places in town to try *cocido a la madrileña* and other favourites such as *callos* (tripe). (p32)

Posada de la Villa Another historical, converted inn where the roasted meats have acquired legend status across the city. (p46)

Tapas bar

acatín A tiled bar
re the *cocido* can be
d as a tapas or the
e authentic all-you-
eat version. (p46)

a Lucio One of
drid's most celebrated
aurants, where
lty and ordinary
drileños eating the
's best *huevos rotos*.
5)

**st for Regional
anish**

ceiras Earthy decor
good down-home
king from the coasts
alicia – *pulpo* (oc-
us) is the prize dish.
3)

Sidrería Vasca Zeraín
Sophisticated Basque
cooking that shows
they're not just obsessed
with tapas up north. (p58)

**La Cocina de María
Luisa** The inland cuisine
of Castilla y León takes
centre stage at this
well-regarded Salamanca
eatery. (p94)

**Restaurante Julián de
Tolosa** The menu at this
fine Navarran institution
is dominated by fabulous
steaks. (p45)

La Paella de la Reina
You could try a seafood
paella, but the Valen-
cian version with rabbit,
chicken and beans is the
most authentic. (p108)

Worth a Trip

Sergi Arola, a
Catalan acolyte of
world-renowned
chef Ferran Adrià,
runs **Sergi Arola
Gastro** (☎91 310 21
69; www.sergiarola
.es; Calle de Zurbano
31; mains €43-52, set
menus €105-135;
⊙lunch & dinner
Mon-Fri, dinner Sat;
Ⓜ Alonso Martínez), a
highly personalised
temple to all that's
innovative in Span-
ish gastronomy.
The menus change
with the seasons;
this is culinary
indulgence at its
finest and booking
well in advance is
necessary.

Best
Tapas

The art of *ir de tapear* (going out for tapas) is one of Madrid's most enduring and best-loved gastronomic and social traditions rolled into one. So many of the city's best tapas bars clamour for space in La Latina, part of a Sunday ritual that has lasted centuries. But such is the local love of tapas that every Madrid *barrio* has some fabulous options. Before setting out, read our detailed exposition on the history and essentials of tapas in the boxed text on p48.

Best for Tapas

Estado Puro Madrid's most innovative tapas from the kitchen lab of masterchef Paco Roncero. (p83)

Taberna Matritum Slightly removed from the main La Latina tapas zone, but worth the slight detour. (p45)

Juana La Loca Wins our vote for Madrid's best *tortilla de patatas* (Spanish omelette). (p45)

La Colonial de Goya Canapés and all manner of alternatives make this one of the best, not just in Salamanca but all Madrid. (p93)

Casa Lucas Thoughtful tapas along Calle de la Cava Baja, Madrid's tapas ground zero. (p41)

Biotza Basque tapas in classy Salamanca surrounds make for a good combination of food and fashion. (p94)

Restaurante Estay A traditional Spanish bar but with a more extensive tapas menu than most. (p89)

Casa Revuelta A Madrid institution for the city's best cod bites, as well as tripe and bacon bits. (p32)

Bocaito Classic Andalucian tapas and bar sta that keep things loud ticking over. (p108)

Albur One of Malasaʼ best tapas bars with a fine restaurant out ba if you feel like a sit-do meal. (p107)

Mercado de San Mig Fresh produce marke meets delicatessen w some of Madrid's mo desirable tapas. (p32)

Best
Cafes

HEMIS/ALAMY ©

drid's thriving cafe culture dates back to the
y and mid-20th centuries when old-style cof-
ouses formed the centrepiece of the coun-
s intellectual life. Many have been lost to time,
some outstanding examples remain and their
ntele long ago broadened to encompass the
re cross-section of modern Madrid society.
hese age-old institutions have been added
ver places that nonetheless serve a similar
pose, at once capturing the purpose of the
drid-cafe-as-meeting-place and evoking the
talgia of the past.

st of the cafes covered here are primarily places
ake a coffee at any hour of the day or early
ning, and we recommend them as such. But
being Spain, the majority stays open well be-
d midnight and they all serve alcohol if you're
eed of something a little stronger.

st Old Literary
fes

é Comercial Marble-
tables and heavy
her chairs make this
doyen of old Madrid
s and literary salons,
t on the Glorieta de
ao. (p109)

**é-Restaurante El
ejo** Another of the
nd old dames of

Madrid high society, this
storied cafe retains its
original decor. (p111)

Gran Café de Gijón The
third in a triumvirate of
cafes that rank among
Europe's best. (p111)

Cafe de Oriente Fabu-
lous palace views and a
stately central European
feel. (p34)

Best Meeting
Places

Café Manuela Old-world
decoration and the lively
hum of modern Madrid –
a perfect mix. (p109)

Café Pepe Botella Bar
meets cafe down on
Plaza Dos de Mayo in the
heart of Malasaña. (p111)

Lolina Vintage Café
One of Malasaña's
coolest retro cafes with
coffee, cocktails and a
mixed Malasaña crowd.
(p103)

Best **Shopping**

Madrid is a great place to shop and shopping in the Spanish capital often involves debunking a few stereotypes in the process. Fashionistas will discover a whole new world of designers and discover in the process that there's so much more to Spanish fashion than Zara and Mango. The buzz surrounding Spanish food and drink is not restricted to the city's restaurants and tapas bars, with some fine purveyors of gourmet foods where you can shop for goodies to carry back home. And then there are the antiques and quality souvenirs that more than compensate for the tacky flamenco dresses and bull T-shirts that can assail visitors at every turn.

Spanish Fashions

Just as Spanish celebrity chefs have taken the world by storm, the world's most prestigious catwalks are clamouring for Spanish designers. The bold colours and eye-catching designs may be relative newcomers on the international stage, but they've been around in Madrid for far longer, with most designers making their names during the outpouring of creativity of *la movida madrileña* in the 1980s.

Gourmet Foods

Madrid's markets have undergone something of a revolution in recent years, transforming themselves into vibrant spaces where you can eat as well as shop. Added to these are the small specialist stores where the packaging is often as exquisite as the tastes on offer.

Antiques & Souvenirs

You *could* buy your friends back home a bullfighting poster with their names on it. Or you could go for a touch more class and take home a lovely papier mâché figurine, a carefully crafted ceramic bowl or a hand-painted Spanish fan.

Best for Spanish Fashions

Agatha Ruiz de la Prada The icon of a generation, Agatha's outrageous colours make her the Pedro Almodóvar of Spanish fashion. (p89)

Camper Only Spanish designers could make a world fashion superstar out of bowling-shoe chic. (p88)

Manolo Blahnik The world-famous maker of designer shoes for celebrities from all corners of the globe. (p89)

Best for Gourmet Foods

Lhardy The upstairs restaurant may be an institution, but the gourmet delicatessen downstairs is its rival in quality. (p56)

Agatha Ruiz de la Prada (p89)

Best for Antiques & Souvenirs

El Arco Artesanía
Designer souvenirs from papier mâché to ceramics and scarves right on Plaza Mayor. (p37)

Antigua Casa Talavera
Ceramics and tileworks with an individual touch from family potters across the Spanish interior. (p37)

Antigüedades Hom
Lovingly restored antique *abanicos* (Spanish fans) made from bone. (p117)

Casa Hernanz
Rope-soled *alpargatas* (espadrilles) footwear that is the souvenir of the Spanish summer. (p37)

Maty
Flamenco dresses and shoes that have the stamp of authenticity. (p37)

cado de San Miguel
ed meats all vacuum-
ed and ready to take
e is just one of the
gs this remodelled
ket does so well.
2)

nbonerías Santa
-style and near-
ect chocolates gift-
pped like works
rt. (p89)

ol Balaguer One of
in's most celebrated
try chefs is also a
colatier par excel-
ce. (p89)

ntequería Bravo
best old-style
nish deli in Madrid.
7)

Worth a Trip
The women's clothing on offer at **Flamenco** (☎ 91 591 30 79; www.flamenco chic.com; Calle de Sagasta 25; ☺ 10am-9pm Mon-Sat; Ⓜ Alonso Martínez), a vibrant and relentlessly creative store, captures the spirit and passion of Spain's best-loved musical genre. Bright colours are the hallmarks of dresses, jackets, tops and other clothing, with a line in equally colourful children's clothing downstairs.

Best
Art

Madrid is one of the great art capitals of the world. The city's astonishing collection of art museums is the legacy of self-aggrandising Spanish royals of centuries past who courted the great painters of the day and built up peerless collections of masterpieces from all across Europe.

The Golden Mile

Few streets on the planet have the artistic pedigree of the Paseo del Prado. Arrayed along (or just set back from) its shores are three of the world's best art galleries, known locally as the Prado, Thyssen and Reina Sofía. Together their collections form a catalogue of breathtaking breadth and richness, spanning the generations of Spanish masters from Goya to Picasso, with all the major European masters thrown in for good measure.

Beyond the Paseo del Prado

In the rush to Madrid's big three art museums, visitors too often neglect (or fail to realise that they're alongside) other galleries that would be major attractions in any other city. These include one of the few places where Goya's paintings remain in their original setting, an art college where all the Spanish greats studied and a gallery devoted entirely to Joaquín Sorolla, one of Spain's most admired painters but little known beyond Spanish shores. And from the Prado and Reina Sofía to the Caixa Forum and Museo Sorolla, the buildings in which these collections hang rank among Madrid's most artistic architectural forms.

Best for Spanish Masters

Museo del Prado Co
for Goya and Velázqu
but stay all day for a j
ney through the riche
centuries of European
art. A worthy rival to t
Louvre – it's that goo
(p66)

Real Academia de Bellas Artes de San Fernando Picasso an
Dalí studied here, and
there are works by Go
Picasso, Velázquez ar
Zurbarán to name jus
some of the househol
names that you'll find
here. (p55)

Ermita de San Anto
de la Florida Extraor
nary frescoes painted
Goya in 1798 remain *i*
situ in this unassumin
little hermitage – one
Madrid's most under-
rated attractions. (p1

Las Meninas (p69) by Velázquez, Museo del Prado

st for
ntemporary Art

**ntro de Arte Reina
ía** Picasso's *Guernica*
d the artist's prepara-
y sketches steal the
ow, but there's also
vador Dalí, Joan Miró
d the leading artists
20th-century Spain.
2)

ixa Forum Avant-
de architecture
ovides the stage for a
h and revolving round
emporary exhibitions
oss a range of genres
t include photography,
nting and installation
(p83)

ería Moriarty An
nic, small and private
drid gallery. (p106)

Best of the Rest

**Museo Thyssen-
Bornemisza** Private
collection that encom-
passes the great names
of European art, begin-
ning in medieval times
and reaching a crescendo
with Jackson Pollock and
Mark Rothko. (p76)

Museo Sorolla Valencian
artist whose paintings
(and former home that
houses them) capture
the essence of the
Mediterranean. (p117)

Museo Lázaro Galdiano
Another stellar private
collection with Goya and
El Greco in a fine old Salamanca mansion. (p86)

**San Lorenzo de El Esco-
rial** El Greco and so many
other minor masters add
art gallery to this palace-
monastery complex's
myriad charms. (p118)

Worth a Trip

Huddled behind
the modern apart-
ment buildings
northwest of Plaza
de España, the
Museo de Cerralbo
(91 547 36 46; http://
museocerralbo.mcu.es;
Calle de Ventura
Rodríguez 17; adult/
concession €3/free, free
Sun, 2-3pm Sat & 5-8pm
Thu; 9.30am-3pm
Tue, Wed, Fri & Sat,
9.30am-3pm & 5-8pm
Thu, 10am-3pm Sun;
Ventura Rodríguez) is
a noble old man-
sion jammed with
everything from
Asian pieces to reli-
gious paintings and
clocks. In the midst
of it all are magnif-
icent artworks by
Zurbarán, Ribera,
Van Dyck and
El Greco.

Best Green Spaces

Once you escape the very heart of downtown Madrid, the city begins to breathe. The most obvious choice for an escape into the greenery is the Parque del Buen Retiro, one of Europe's loveliest parks and monumental gardens, but there are plenty of other options. The footpaths running down the middle of the Paseo del Prado are gloriously shady, presided over by trees planted in the 18th century, and lined on one side by the Real Jardín Botánico, Madrid's botanical gardens. And west of the centre, the lovely Parque del Oeste drops down the hill from the *barrio* of Argüelles, Campo de Moro extends out behind the Palacio Real and the Casa de Campo is a vast stand of greenery even further away to the west.

Best Parks

Parque del Buen Retiro Madrid's loveliest and largest stand of green, littered with monuments and filled with empty lawns. (p80)

Jardines de Sabatini Manicured gardens in the shadow of the Palacio Real, with fountains and maze-like hedges. (p27)

Plaza de Olavide One of Madrid's greenest squares with shaded bars around the perimeter. (p117)

Best Beyond the Centre

Casa de Campo (M Batán) A vast area of parkland that's hugely popular on weekends with restaurants, a cable car, lake, zoo and fun park.

Campo de Moro (Paseo de la Virgen del Puerto; 10am-8pm Mon-Sat, 9am-8pm Sun & holidays Apr-Sep, 10am-6pm; M Príncipe Pío) The Retiro's rival for the title of Madrid's loveliest park – it's hidden down the hill behind the royal palace.

Best
For Kids

e all major cities, Madrid requires you to plan
efully to make sure that your children enjoy
ir visit to the city as much as you do. The
or art galleries sometimes have activities for
dren, while most also have printed guides
igned for them. Playgrounds also inhabit many
squares – ask the tourist office if they know
nearest one. In addition to playgrounds, the
que del Buen Retiro has a host of child-centric
vities on offer. If you're willing to travel a little
ond the centre, the Casa de Campo has a zoo,
usement park and a cable car to help you get
re. A visit to Real Madrid's football stadium
also hold great appeal for children of a certain
. And remember that Madrid is an extremely
d-friendly city in the sense that children will
welcome in most bars and all but the most
nal restaurants, with waiters usually happy to
r suggestions for meals. An increasing (though
small) number of restaurants have children's
nus.

CARLOS DOMINIQUE/ALAMY ©

st for Kids

que del Buen Retiro
p p82, C3; ⊙6am-
ight May-Sep, to 11pm
Apr; M Retiro, Príncipe
ergara, Ibiza, Atocha)
ygrounds, vast open
ces, boat rides, bike
and occasional pup-
shows.

**Aquarium de
drid** (⊘902 345014;
.zoomadrid.com; Casa
ampo; adult/child
35/17.60; ⊙10.30am-

8.30pm Jul & Aug, reduced
hrs Sep-Jun; 🚍37 from
Intercambiador de Príncipe
Pío, M Casa de Campo) An
attractive zoo with a full
range of species.

Parque de Atracciones
(⊘91 463 29 00; www
.parquedeatracciones.es;
Casa de Campo; >120cm/
90-120cm/<90cm €29.90/
23.90/free; ⊙noon-midnight
Sun-Fri, noon-1am Sat Jul &
Aug, reduced hrs Sep-Jun;
🚍37 from Intercambiador

de Príncipe Pío, M Batán) A
good amusement park
with plenty of rides for
all ages.

Teleférico (⊘91 541 11 18;
www.teleferico.com; one-way/
return €3.75/5.50; ⊙noon-
9pm Mon-Fri, noon-9.30pm
Sat & Sun Jun-Aug, reduced
hrs Sep-May; M Argüelles) A
cable car connecting the
Paseo de Pinto Rosales to
Casa de Campo.

**Estadio Santiago Berna-
béu** (⊘902 291709, 91 398
43 00; www.realmadrid.com;
Ave de Concha Espina 1; tour
adult/child €16/11; ⊙10am-
7pm Mon-Sat, 10.30am-
6.30pm Sun, except match
days; M Santiago Bernabéu)
Real Madrid's home and
one of the most impres-
sive football stadiums
on earth, with tours, a
museum, and matches
from August to May.

Best
Bars

Nights in the Spanish capital are the stuff of legend and what Hemingway wrote of the city in the 1930s remains true to this day: 'Nobody goes to bed in Madrid until they have killed the night.' Madrid has more bars than any city in the world, six, in fact, for every 100 inhabitants and wherever you are in town, there'll be a bar close by.

If you're unaccustomed to Madrid's late eating hours, the upside is that it allows plenty of time for a pre-dinner drink and it's an activity that locals have turned into an institution. Of course, they often combine the two – eating and drinking – by starting early with a drink and some tapas. So in addition to the bars we cover in these lists, it's always worth considering those places better known for their food when planning your first step into the night because they're often terrific places to drink as well.

Madrid's bars range from simple, local watering holes that serve as centres of community life to sophisticated temples to good taste. The former usually open throughout the day, while the latter rarely do so before 8pm. Otherwise, some places may close half an hour earlier or later (especially on Friday and Saturday nights), but 3am operates as a threshold.

The hours between midnight and 3am are filled with choices, although we recommend that you take up residence in one of the oh-so-cool cocktail bars.

Best Cocktail Bars

Museo Chicote Madrid's most famous cocktail bar beloved by celebrities from Hemingway to Sophia Loren. (p109)

Del Diego A quieter venue for A-list *famosos* and near-perfect (and always creative) cocktails. (p111)

El Eucalipto Cuba lives and breathes down in Lavapiés with some of Madrid's best mojitos. (p47)

Rooftop Bars

La Terraza del Urban The height of class on a warm summer's evening. (p59)

The Penthouse Slick venue high above Plaza de Santa Ana with sky-high admission prices to match. (p53)

The Penthouse (p53)

udeamus Café Cool
casual bar alongside
Lavapiés rooftops.
6)

d Barrio Bars

Venencia A tímeless
rry bar where old
rels abound close
Plaza de Santa Ana.
8)

dega de la Ardosa
ther neighbourhood
ssic north of the
tre. (p117)

st of the Rest

mperfecto Great
ktails and a real Huer-
buzz make this one of
drid's best bars. (p59)

fé del Real Possibly
favourite bar down-
n, especially on the
tairs stools. (p34)

Taberna Alhambra One
of the best and busiest
bars close to Sol, with a
real cross-section of the
Madrid night in attend-
ance. (p59)

Taberna Tempranillo A
great La Latina wine bar
along Calle de la Cava
Baja, with an entire wall
of wine bottles. (p47)

Café del Nuncio Rome
and Madrid rolled into
one, tumbling down the
steps. (p46)

Café Pepe Botella A brilliant Malasaña bar right
on Plaza Dos de Mayo,
the *barrio*'s heartbeat.
(p111)

Anticafé Bohemian
decor and an alternative
slant on life. (p35)

Worth a Trip

Overlooking
one of the most
famous football
fields on earth, the
**Real Café Berna-
béu** (☎91 458 36 67;
www.realcafebernabeu
.es; Gate 30, Estadio
Santiago Bernabéu,
Avenida de Concha
Espina; ⏰9pm-1am;
Ⓜ Santiago Bernabéu)
is a trendy cocktail
bar with excep-
tional views and a
steady stream of
beautiful people
among the clien-
tele. It closes two
hours before a
game and doesn't
open until an
hour after.

Best
Live Music &
Flamenco

Madrid has a happening live-music scene, which owes a lot to the city's role as the cultural capital of the Spanish-speaking world. There's flamenco, world-class jazz and a host of performers you may never have heard of – one of whom may just be Spain's next big thing. For something more edifying, there's opera and *zarzuela*.

Flamenco

Flamenco's roots lie in Andalucía, but the top performers gravitate towards Madrid for live performances; keep your ear to the ground in case one of the city's flamenco festivals is on while you're in town. Remember also that most *tablaos* (flamenco venues) offer meals to go with the floorshow. In our experience, the meals are often overpriced, but if you just pay for the show (the admission usually includes a drink) you may not have the best seat in the house. If possible, go to the venue in person to buy your ticket to get a sense of where you'll be seated.

Jazz

Madrid has some of Europe's best jazz with at least three fine venues, one of which was voted one of the world's best not so long ago. Groups often play for a whole week, making it easier to get tickets.

Rock Madrid

At the height of *la movida madrilèna*, the crazy outpouring of creativity and hedonism in Madrid in the 1980s, an estimated 300 rock bands were performing in the bars of Malasaña alone. There aren't quite so many these days, but there are still plenty that capture that spirit.

Best Flamenco

Las Tablas A smaller, more intimate venue v consistently high-qual performances. (p35)

Casa Patas One of M drid's most celebrated flamenco stages, with a respected flamenco school attached. (p47

Villa Rosa Once appeared in an Almodóva movie and has recentl returned to its flamen roots. (p60)

Cardamomo A dimly lit bar where the performances rank amon Madrid's best. (p61)

Café de Chinitas A fi stage with an elegant setting. (p35)

Best Jazz

Café Central Regular ranked among the elit world jazz clubs; all th

Populart (p53)

names have played
neath the fabulous art
o decor. (p60)

pulart A more earthy
d free) venue, but the
s here are often the
l of Café Central, its
re illustrious neigh-
ur up the road. (p53)

Berlín Jazz Café An-
er classic jazz stage
t gets high marks
m purists for never
aying too far from
ditional jazz. (p35)

Junco Jazz Club Live
z then dancing all
nt: it's a fine combina-
n. (p111)

st Rock &
e Rest

a El Sol One of the
ends of 1980s Madrid
d still going strong.
0)

**Costello Café & Nite-
club** A sophisticated
venue that feels like a
SoHo cocktail bar. (p61)

Nasti Club The essence
of Malasaña with a
grungy feel and up-and-
coming bands. (p103)

Best High Culture

Teatro Real Spain's
finest opera perform-
ers take to the stage at
this acoustically perfect
venue. (p36)

Teatro de la Zarzuela
Madrid's very own cross
between theatre and
opera; the theatre also
hosts the finest in con-
temporary dance. (p60)

Worth a Trip

Honky Tonk (☎91
445 61 91; www.club
honky.com; Calle de
Covarrubias 24; admis-
sion free; ⏱9pm-5am;
Ⓜ Alonso Martínez)
is a great place to
see blues or local
rock 'n' roll, though
many acts have a
little country, jazz
or R&B thrown into
the mix, too. It's a
fun vibe in a small-
ish club that's been
around since the
heady 1980s and
opens 365 days a
year.

Best
Clubs

Madrid nights are long and loud and people here live fully for the moment. Today's encounter can be tomorrow's distant memory, perhaps in part because Madrid's nightclubs (also known as *discotecas*) rival any in the world. The best places are usually the megaclubs with designer decor, designer people and, sometimes, with enough space for numerous dance floors each with their own musical style to suit your mood. Themed nights are all the rage, so it's always worth checking in advance to see what flavour of the night takes your fancy. Although you'll find a nightclub going strong until sunrise in almost every *barrio*, the biggest selection of clubs are to be found downtown.

Most nightclubs don't open their doors until around midnight, don't really get going until after 1am, and some won't even bat an eyelid until 3am, when the bars elsewhere have closed. Admission prices vary widely, but the standard admission costs around €12. Even those that let you in for free will play catch-up with hefty prices for drinks, so don't plan your night around looking for the cheapest ticket.

Best Clubs
Teatro Joy Eslava
Enduringly popular converted theatre with great music, live acts and a fun crowd. (p35)

Kapital Madrid's megaclub of longest standing with seven floors and something for everyone. (p83)

Cool Sleek curves – a that's just the clientel themed nights from Thursday to Saturday (p36)

Almonte Flamenco tunes and a formidab cast of amateur flamenco wannabes ma for an alternative slan the night. (p95)

Serrano 41 Keep you eyes peeled for the Re Madrid set; it has a to door policy as you'd expect. (p95)

Why Not? Chueca's favourite nightclub regardless of your sex orientation. (p112)

Best
Gay & Lesbian

…drid has always been one of Europe's most …-friendly cities. The city's gay community is …dited with reinvigorating the once down-at-…l inner-city *barrio* of Chueca, where Madrid …n't just come out of the closet, it ripped the …rs off in the process. Today the *barrio* is one …Madrid's most vibrant and it's very much the …rt and soul of gay Madrid. Cafes, bars and …htclubs clearly oriented to a gay clientele …ound, and book, video and adult-toy shops …ed at gay people continue to spring up in and …und Chueca, as well as gay-friendly hostels. … there's nothing ghetto-like about Chueca. …extravagantly gay and lesbian personality is …thing but exclusive and the crowd is almost …ays mixed gay–straight. As gay and lesbian …dents like to say, Chueca isn't gay-friendly, … hetero-friendly.

…a great time to be gay in Madrid. Under laws …sed by the Spanish Congress in 2005, same-sex …rriages now enjoy the same legal protection …hose between heterosexual partners. Opinion …s at the time showed that the reforms were …ported by more than two-thirds of Spaniards.

KRZYSZTOF DYDYNSKI/GETTY IMAGES ©

Black & White Few venues have the history of this place; it's been here since Chueca turned gay. Expect cabaret and just about anything else. (p112)

Cool One of Madrid's coolest nightclubs, as the name suggests, it's all very amorous and gay on Saturday nights in particular. (p36)

…st Gay & Lesbian

…é Acuarel A huge,
…le male statue
…rds the doorway at
… agreeable, dimly lit
…on centrepiece of gay
…drid (p109)

Why Not? Almost anything goes at this reliably intimate nightclub where gay and straight couples merge seamlessly (p112)

Best
For Free

Museo del Prado It's free from 6pm to 8pm Monday to Saturday and from 5pm to 7pm Sunday. Not necessarily the best times to visit Spain's best art gallery as crowds can overwhelm, but it can be a good option if you're on you're second or third visit or simply counting your euros. (p66)

Centro de Arte Reina Sofía Free on Sunday – again, it might be worth paying at other times to avoid the crowds but *Guernica* for free is, well, priceless. (p72)

Ermita de San Antonio de la Florida No such problems here, as Goya's frescoes are free every day that the museum is open. (p114)

Caixa Forum The exhibitions at this vibrant museum-cum-cultural-centre may not always appeal, but it costs nothing to take a look to see if do they appeal. (p83)

Museo Sorolla Tucked away in the Madrid *barrio* of Chamberí, the free admission hours here on Sunday rarely attract a crowd. (p117)

Plaza de Toros & Museo Taurino If you don't want to watch a bullfight (for which you do pay) or don't take a tour (ditto), consider a free visit to the bullring and its museum. (p98)

Estación de Chamberí Take a journey underground to Madrid's ghost metro station, now a museum and tickets (free) are a whole cheaper than taking the train. (p117)

Templo de Debod Madrid's very own Egyptian temple doesn't cost a cent, nor does the lovely parkland that surrounds it. (p115)

Museo al Aire Libre Outdoor sculptures by some of Spain's best-known artists sit beneath an overpass along Paseo de la Castellana. (p92)

☑ **Top Tip**

▶ South of the centre and next to the revamped Madrid riverfront, **Matadero Madrid** (☏91 252 52 53; www.mataderomadrid.com; Paseo de la Chopera 14; admission free; ☺4-10pm Tue-Fri, 11am-10pm Sat & Sun; Ⓜ Legazpi) is a stunning contemporary arts centre that occupies the converted buildings of an old livestock market and slaughterhouse. It hosts cutting-edge drama, musical and dance performances and exhibitions.

Survival Guide

Survival Guide

Before You Go

When to Go

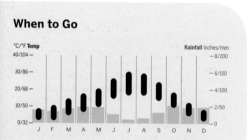

°C/°F Temp
40/104 —
30/86 —
20/68 —
10/50 —
0/32 —

Rainfall Inches/mm
— 8/200
— 6/150
— 4/100
— 2/50
— 0

J F M A M J J A S O N D

➡ **Summer (Jun-Aug)**
Can be fiercely hot; many locals desert the city; in August, many restaurants close and sights operate on reduced hours.

➡ **Autumn (Sep-Nov)**
Nice time to visit with mild temperatures; warmish in September, cool in November.

➡ **Winter (Dec-Feb)**
Can be bitterly cold; snow possible but often clear skies; Christmas is a festive time in the city; flamenco festival in February.

➡ **Spring (Mar-May)**
Mild temperatures; Semana Santa (Easter) and May festivals.

Book Your Stay

➡ In Madrid, a *habitación doble* (double room) ally indicates a room two single beds; cud couples should reque *cama de matrimonio* ally, a marriage bed).

➡ Royal Madrid and anywhere around Sol La Latina and Huerta puts you within walkin distance of most sigh and plenty of restaura but it can be noisy.

➡ Salamanca and the Paseo del Prado tend be more upmarket an generally quieter.

➡ Malasaña and Chue are a little removed fr the major sights (it's all relative – you're st walking distance away but they offer fascina insights into local life.

➡ Be wary of high sea (*temporada alta*), whi Madrid can depend m on trade fairs than the weather.

he budget end of
arket, there are
 of backpacker
 with dorms and
hostales with
e bathrooms.

range is where
s the widest variety
ice, with charming
onal architecture
rted into chic
er hotels.

he top end of the
et, the sky's the limit
it comes to luxury
ice, with refined
 valuing old-world
ce as well as inno-
temples to modern
.

ays check when
ving your room, but
eneral rule all but
ost basic *hostales*
free internet access,
 wireless or a com-
in the lobby.

ul Websites

y Planet (www
planet.com) Author
nmendations and
 booking.

tasol (www.apartasol
Apartments around
entre.

n Madrid (www
madrid.es) Long- and
-stay apartments.

Best Budget

Cat's Hostel (www.cats
hostel.com) Lovely patio
and real backpacker vibe.

Mad Hostel (www.mad
hostel.com) Smallish
dorms but a great all-
round package.

Hostal Horizonte (www
.hostalhorizonte.com) Old-
style welcome in this
traveller-run *hostal*.

Hostal Madrid (www
.hostalmadrid.com) Rooms
and apartments at this
friendly central option.

Hostal Luis XV (www
.hrluisxv.net) Good rooms
and fabulous views from
the 8th floor.

**Los Amigos Sol
Backpackers Hostel**
(www.losamigoshostel.com)
Traveller-savvy place to
meet other backpackers.

Best Midrange

Hotel Meninas (www
.hotelmeninas.com) Cool
and classy place that
rates highly on traveller
surveys.

Hotel Plaza Mayor
(www.h-plazamayor.com)
Hard to be more central,
with lovely attic rooms
the pick.

Hotel Alicia (www
.room-matehoteles.com)
The best of the excellent
Room Mate chain in
Madrid.

Chic & Basic Colours
(www.chicandbasic.com)
A designer look at
lower midrange prices in
Huertas.

Praktik Metropol (www
.hotelpraktikmetropol.com)
Fun and funky rooms high
above Madrid.

Hotel Ábalu (www
.hotelabalu.com) A stylish
place at the happening
end of Malasaña.

Best Top End

Hotel Urban (www.derby
hotels.com) Classy and
achingly modern in all the
right places.

Me by Meliá (www
.memadrid.com) Fabulous
front-row rooms over-
looking Plaza de Santa
Ana.

Hotel Ritz (www.ritz
madrid.com) Unrivalled
old-world luxury next to
the Museo del Prado.

Westin Palace (www
.westinpalacemadrid.com)
One of the most pres-
tigious luxury hotels in
town.

Casa de Madrid (www
.casademadrid.com) A per-
sonal touch with Ritz-like
luxury.

Hotel Puerta América
(www.hotelpuertamerica
.com) Architect-designed
rooms on the road in
from the airport.

Arriving in Madrid

From Aeropuerto de Barajas

➜ **Metro** (one-way €4.50; ⊙6.05am-2am; 15-25 min; line 8) Runs to the Nuevos Ministerios transport interchange, which connects with lines 10 and 6. Buy tickets at the airport station.

➜ **Bus** The Exprés Aeropuerto (Airport Express; www.emtmadrid.es; €5, 40 minutes; ⊙24hr) runs between Puerta de Atocha train station and the airport. From 11.55pm until 5.35am, departures are from the Plaza de la Cibeles, not the train station.

➜ **Taxi** A taxi to the centre (around 30 minutes, depending on traffic) costs €25 to €35.

From Estación de Atocha

➜ **Metro** (one-way/ten-trip ticket €1.50/12; ⊙6am-1am; line 1) From Atocha Renfe station to Sol (10 to 15 minutes) with connections elsewhere via lines 2 and 3. Buy tickets from machines at the station.

➜ **Taxi** A taxi to the centre (around 10 minutes, depending on traffic) costs around €5 to €7.

From Estación de Chamartín

➜ **Metro** (one-way/ten-trip ticket €1.50/12; ⊙6am-1am, lines 1 & 10) From Chamartín station to Sol (15 to 20 minutes) with connections elsewhere via lines 2 and 3. Buy tickets from machines at the station.

➜ **Taxi** A taxi to the centre (around 15 minutes, depending on traffic) costs around €10.

☑ **Top Tip** For the best way to get to your accommodation, see p17.

Getting Around

Metro

☑ **Best for...** Madrid's metro is almost always the best choice, with an extensive network of lines and stations throughout the city.

➜ **Metro de Madrid** (www.metromadrid.es) Runs a metro system with 12 colour-coded lines.

➜ Single tickets, goo[d] one journey no mat[ter] how many changes [you] have to make, cost [€1.50] and can be bought a[t] metro stations.

➜ The metro operate[s] from 6.05am to 2a[m,] although there is ta[lk] of shutting it down a[t] midnight.

Bus

☑ **Best for...** Night [travel] when the metro shu[ts] down, for those for w[hom] metro stairs are imp[ossi]ble (eg people with p[rams,] travellers with disabi[lities]) and to see a little of [Ma]drid above ground as [you] get around.

➜ **EMT buses** (www.e[mt]madrid.es) Travel alon[g] most city routes reg[ularly] between about 6.30[am] and 11.30pm.

➜ Twenty-six night-b[us] *búhos* (owls) routes [also] operate from 11.45p[m to] 5.30am, with all rou[tes] originating in Plaza [de] Cibeles.

➜ Fares for day and n[ight] trips are the same: €[1.50] for a single trip, €12 [for a] 10-trip Metrobús tic[ket.] Single-trip tickets ca[n be] purchased on board.

ckets & sses

-trip Metrobús
ets will save you
e and money
are sold in ma-
nes at all metro
tions, as well as
st newspaper
sks and *estancos*
bacconists).
0-trip ticket
2) is valid on
metro and EMT
ses. An *Abono
nsporte Turístico
urist Ticket;
1/2/7 days
/13.40/33.40) is
o possible.

anías

st for...** Getting
Lorenzo de El
al, or a quick
-south trip between
artín and Atocha
tations (with stops
evos Ministerios
ol).

short-range
nías trains operated
nfe (www.renfe.es/
ias/madrid) go places
he metro doesn't.

kets range between
and €8 depend-
how far you're
ling.

Taxi

☑ **Best for...** Quick trips
across town outside peak
hour.

➡ Taxis are reasonably
priced and charges are
posted on the inside of
passenger-side windows.
The trip from Sol to the
Museo del Prado costs
about €5.

➡ You can call a taxi at
Tele-Taxi (☎ 91 371 21 31;
www.tele-taxi.es) and **Radio-
Teléfono Taxi** (☎ 91 547 82
00; www.radiotelefono-taxi
.com) or flag one down in
the street.

Essential Information

Business Hours

Reviews in this guidebook
don't list business hours
unless they differ from
the following standards:

➡ **Banks** 8.30am to 2pm
Monday to Friday; some
also open 4pm to 7pm
Thursday and 9am to
1pm Saturday.

➡ **Central Post Offices**
8.30am to 9.30pm Mon-
day to Friday, 8.30am to
2pm Saturday.

➡ **Restaurants** Lunch
1pm to 4pm, dinner 8pm
to midnight.

➡ **Shops** 10am to 2pm
and 4.30pm to 7.30pm or
5pm to 8pm.

Discount Cards

➡ Student cards offer
discounts of up to 50% at
many sights.

➡ If you're over 65, you
may be eligible for an
admission discount to
some attractions.

➡ If you intend to do
some intensive sightsee-
ing and travelling on
public transport, it might
be worth looking at the
Madrid Card (☎ 91 360
47 72; www.madridcard.com;
1/2/3 days adult €39/49/59,
child age 6-12 €20/28/34).
It includes free entry to
more than 40 museums
in and around Madrid.

➡ If you plan to visit the
Museo del Prado, Museo
Thyssen-Bornemisza
and Centro de Arte Reina
Sofía while in Madrid,
the Paseo del Arte ticket
covers them all in a com-
bined ticket for €21.60
and is valid for one visit
to each gallery during a
12-month period; buying
separate tickets would
cost €27.

Electricity

220V/230V/50Hz

Emergency

Servicio de Atención al Turista Extranjero (Foreign Tourist Assistance Service; ☎ 902 10 21 12, 91 548 85 37, 91 548 80 08; www .esmadrid.com/satemadrid; Calle de Leganitos 19; ☉ 9am-10pm; Ⓜ Plaza de España, Santo Domingo) Specially trained officers can assist with contacting your embassy or your family, as well as cancelling credit cards.

Ambulance (☎ 061)
EU standard emergency number (☎ 112)
Fire Brigade (Bomberos; ☎ 080)
National Police (Policía Nacional; ☎ 091)

Money

Currency Euro (€)
ATMs Widely available; usually a charge on ATM cash withdrawals abroad
Cash Banks and building societies offer the best rates; take your passport
Credit cards Accepted in most hotels, restaurants and shops; may need to show passport or other photo ID
Tipping Small change in restaurants, round up to the nearest euro in taxis

Public Holidays

Many shops are closed and many attractions operate on reduced hours on the following dates:
Año Nuevo (New Year's Day) 1 January
Reyes (Epiphany or Three Kings' Day) 6 January
Jueves Santo (Holy Thursday) March/April
Viernes Santo (Good Friday) March/April
Fiesta del Trabajo (Labour Day) 1 May
Fiesta de la Comunidad de Madrid 2 May
Fiestas de San Isidro Labrador 15 May
La Asunción (Feast of the Assumption) 15 August
Día de la Hispanidad (Spanish National Day) 12 October

Money-Saving Tips

➡ Look out for free entry at sights (see p144)
➡ Order the *menú del día* for lunch in restaurants
➡ Buy discount car (see p149)
➡ Buy 10-trip travel cards to get around the city (see p149)

Día de Todos los Santos (All Saints' Day) 1 November
Día de la Virgen de la Almudena 9 November
Día de la Constitución (Constitution Day) 6 December
La Inmaculada Concepción (Feast of the Immaculate Conception) 8 December
Navidad (Christmas) 25 December

Safe Travel

Petty crime and theft, with tourists as the prey of choice, is a problem in Madrid, although most visitors encounter few problems. Take particular care on the metro, at the El Rastro Sunday morning flea market, around attractions popular with tourists (such as the Museo del Prado

hone

Phones

SIM cards are
available and can
d in European
stralian mobile
s. Other phones
eed to be set to
g.

Codes

ational access
$\square$00)

country code

Numbers

ational directory
ies ($\square$11825)

ational operator
erse charges
t) Europe ($\square$1008);
world ($\square$1005)

os &
on'ts

reet people with
full 'Hola, bue-
días' (morning)
Hola, buenas
des' (afternoon).

a social setting,
customary to
et people with a
s on each cheek,
hough two men
only do this if
se friends.

Toilets

Public toilets are almost
nonexistent in Madrid and
it's not really the done
thing to go into a bar or
cafe solely to use the toi-
let; ordering a quick coffee
is a small price to pay.

Tourist
Information

The Madrid government's
**Centro de Turismo de
Madrid** ($\square$91 588 16 36;
www.esmadrid.com; Plaza
Mayor 27; ⊙9.30am-8.30pm;
MSol) is terrific. Among
other services (including
guided tours of the city),
it offers free downloads
of the metro map to your
mobile.

There's a smaller
tourist office (Plaza de
Colón; ⊙9.30am-8.30pm;
MColón), which is acces-
sible via the underground
stairs on the corner of
Calle de Goya and Paseo
de la Castellana.

Smaller, bright orange
tourist information points
can be found at the fol-
lowing locations:

➡ **Plaza de la Cibeles**
(Plaza de la Cibeles;
⊙9.30am-8.30pm; **M**Banco
de España)

➡ **Plaza del Callao** (Plaza
del Callao; ⊙9am-midnight;
MCallao)

➡ **Paseo del Arte** (cnr
Calle de Santa Isabel

& Plaza del Emperador
Carlos V; ⊙9.30am-8.30pm;
MAtocha)

➡ **Aeropuerto de
Barajas** (Barajas Airport;
T4; ⊙9am-8pm; **M**Aero-
puerto T4)

Travellers with
Disabilities

Although things are
slowly changing, Madrid
remains something of
an obstacle course for
travellers with a disability.
Your first stop for more
information on accessibil-
ity for travellers should be
the Madrid tourist office
website section known as
Madrid Accesible (www
.esmadrid.com), where you
can download a list of
wheelchair-accessible
hotels, and a pdf called
'Lugares Accesibles', a
list of wheelchair-friendly
restaurants, shopping
centres and museums.

Visas

➡ Citizens or residents
of EU & Schengen coun-
tries: no visa required.

➡ Citizens or residents of
Australia, Canada, Israel,
Japan, NZ and the USA:
no visa required for tourist visits of up to 90 days.

➡ Other countries: check
with a Spanish embassy
or consulate.

Language

Spanish (*español*) – often referred to as *castellano* (Castilian) to distinguish it from other languages spoken in Spain – is the language of Madrid. While you'll find an increasing number of *madrileños* who speak some English, especially younger people and hotel and restaurant employees, don't count on it. Travellers who learn a little Spanish will be amply rewarded as Spaniards appreciate the effort, no matter how basic your understanding of the language.

Most Spanish sounds are pronounced the same as their English counterparts. Just read our pronunciation guides as if they were English and you'll be understood. Note that 'm/f' indicates masculine and feminine forms.

To enhance your trip with a phrasebook, visit **lonelyplanet.com**. Lonely Planet iPhone phrasebooks are available through the Apple App store.

Basics

Hello.
Hola.   o·la

Goodbye.
Adiós.   a·dyos

How are you?
¿Qué tal?   ke tal

Fine, thanks.
Bien, gracias.   byen gra·thyas

Please.
Por favor.   por fa·vor

Thank you.
Gracias.   gra·thyas

Excuse me.
Perdón.   per·don

Sorry.
Lo siento.   lo syen·to

Yes./No.
Sí./No.   see/no

Do you speak (English)?
¿Habla (inglés)?   a·bla (een·gles)

I (don't) understand.
Yo (no) entiendo.   yo (no) en·tyen

What's your name?
¿Cómo se   ko·mo se
llama?   lya·ma

My name is ...
Me llamo ...   me lya·mo ...

Eating & Drinking

Can I see the menu, please?
¿Puedo ver el   pwe·do ver el
menu, por favor?   me·noo por fa·v

I'm a vegetarian. (m/f)
Soy   soy
vegetariano/a.   ve·khe·ta·rya·no

Cheers!
¡Salud!   sa·loo

That was delicious!
¡Estaba   es·ta·ba
buenísimo!   bwe·nee·see·me

The bill, please.
La cuenta,   la kwen·ta
por favor.   por fa·vor

I'd like ...
Quisiera ...   kee·sye·ra ...

a coffee	*un café*	oon ka·fe
a table for two	*una mesa para dos*	oo·na me pa·ra dos
a wine	*un vino*	oon vee·ı
two beers	*dos cervezas*	dos ther·ve·tl

ping

to buy ...
a kee·sye·ra
ar ... kom·prar ...

ook at it?
o verlo? pwe·do ver·lo

uch is it?
o cuesta? kwan·to kwes·ta

very expensive.
caro. es mooy ka·ro

u lower the price?
a bajar po·dree·a ba·khar
o oon po·ko
o? el pre·thyo

gencies

ro! so·ko·ro

doctor!
a lya·me a oon
ico! me·dee·ko

e police!
a lya·me a
ía! la po·lee·thee·a

t. (m/f)
erdido/a. es·toy per·dee·do/a

(m/f)
nfermo/a. es·toy en·fer·mo/a

are the toilets?
 están don·de es·tan
os? los ba·nyos

& Numbers

ime is it?
ora es? ke o·ra es

) o'clock.
s diez). son (las dyeth)

g mañana ma·nya·na
oon tarde tar·de
g noche no·che

yesterday	ayer	a·yer
today	hoy	oy
tomorrow	mañana	ma·nya·na
1	uno	oo·no
2	dos	dos
3	tres	tres
4	cuatro	kwa·tro
5	cinco	theen·ko
6	seis	seys
7	siete	sye·te
8	ocho	o·cho
9	nueve	nwe·ve
10	diez	dyeth

Transport & Directions
Where's ...?
¿Dónde está ...? don·de es·ta ...

Where's the station?
¿Dónde está don·de es·ta
la estación? la es·ta·thyon

What's the address?
¿Cuál es la kwal es la
dirección? dee·rek·thyon

Can you show me (on the map)?
¿Me lo puede me lo pwe·de
indicar een·dee·kar
(en el mapa)? (en el ma·pa)

I want to go to ...
Quisiera ir a ... kee·sye·ra eer a ...

What time does it arrive/leave?
¿A qué hora a ke o·ra
llega/sale? lye·ga/sa·le

Please tell me when we get to ...
¿Puede avisarme pwe·de a·vee·sar·me
cuando lleguemos kwan·do lye·ge·mos
a ...? a ...

I want to get off here.
Quiero bajarme kye·ro ba·khar·me
aquí. a·kee

Behind the Scenes

Send Us Your Feedback

We love to hear from travellers – your comments help make our books better. We read every word, and we guarantee that your feedback goes straight to the autho Visit **lonelyplanet.com/contact** to submit your updates and suggestions.

Note: We may edit, reproduce and incorporate your comments in Lonely Plane products such as guidebooks, websites and digital products, so let us know if you don't want your comments reproduced or your name acknowledged. For a copy c our privacy policy visit lonelyplanet.com/privacy.

Our Readers

Many thanks to the travellers who used the last edition and wrote to us with helpful hints, useful advice and interesting anecdotes:

Selma Algra, Clotilde Farah, Nicola Guaran, Michael Tompkins

Anthony's Thanks

During a decade of living in Madrid, I have been welcomed and assisted by many people whose lives and stories have become a treasured part of the fabric of my own. And to my wife, Marina, and my daughters, Carlota ar Valentina: truly you are Madrid's great est gifts of all.

Acknowledgments

Cover photograph: Plaza Mayor, Madr Alan Copson/AWL-images.

This Book

This 3rd edition of Lonely Planet's *Pocket Madrid* guidebook was researched and written by Anthony Ham, who also wrote the previous two editions. This guidebook was commissioned in Lonely Planet's London office, and produced by the following: **Commissioning Editor** Dora Whitaker **Coordinating**

Editor Nigel Chin **Coordinating Cartographer** James Leversha **Coordinating Layout Designer** Clara Monitto **Managing Editors** Barbara Delissen, Brigitte Ellemor, Martine Power **Managing Cartographers** Shahara Ahmed, Amanda Sierp **Managing Layout Designer** Jane Hart **Assisting Editor** Amanda Williamson **Cover Research** Naomi Parker

Internal Image Researc Claire Gibson **Language Content** Samantha Forge **Thanks to** Liz Abbott, Da Austin, Anita Banh, Laura Crawford, Tobias Gattine Chris Girdler, Ryan Evans Asha Ioculari, Jouve Indi Annelies Mertens, Anna Metcalfe, Trent Paton, Av Robertson, Fiona Sisema Branislava Vladisavljevic Diana Von Holdt, Gerard Walker

See also separate subindexes for:

✖ **Eating p157**

🍷 **Drinking p158**

✪ **Entertainment p158**

🏠 **Shopping p158**

Sights p000
Map Pages **p000**

⊗ Eating

A
Albur 107
Almendro 13 41
Al-Mounia 95

B
Bar La Ideal 34
Bar Palentino 103
Biotza 94
Bocaito 108
Bodega de la Ardosa
   108

Our Writer

Anthony Ham

In 2001, Anthony fell in love with Madrid on his first v
to the city. Less than a year later, he arrived on a one-
ticket with not a word of Spanish and not knowing a s
person. Having recently passed the 10-year mark in M
he now lives in an apartment overlooking his favourit
square in Madrid with his Madrid-born wife and daug
He still adores his adopted city as much as the first d
arrived. When he's not writing for Lonely Planet, Anth
writes about and photographs Spain, Africa and the M
East for newspapers and magazines around the worl

Published by Lonely Planet Publications Pty Ltd
ABN 36 005 607 983
3rd edition – Jan 2013
ISBN 978 1 74179 955 2
© Lonely Planet 2013   Photographs © as indicated 2013
10 9 8 7 6 5 4 3 2 1
Printed in China